ANNE FRANK IN THE WORLD

DIE WELT DER ANNE FRANK

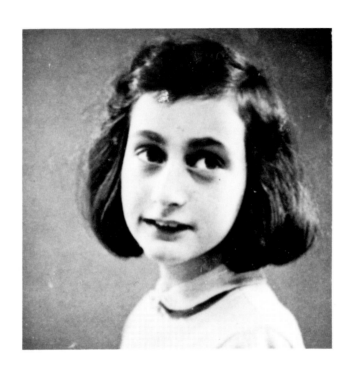

ANNE FRANK STICHTING

UITGEVERIJ BERT BAKKER AMSTERDAM

ANNE FRANK IN THE WORLD

1929

1945

DIE WELT DER ANNE FRANK

PREFACE

Had Anne Frank, a typical child, lived next door, could she have counted on us for help during the Nazi regime?

Would we have recognized the dangers of fascism, or would we have believed the propaganda that depicted Jews as inferior, untrustworthy citizens? Would we have agreed with those who singled out the Jews as the cause of all evil – just as some people today feel free to blame 'the foreigners' for all their ills?

Or would we have continued – perhaps with a feeling of powerlessness – our daily routine?

Many Germans did, in fact, continue their daily routine. They were not alone. The Dutch and other people, as well, acted in the same way without even being aware of their action, or – as it turns out – their lack of action. This indifference, this resignation, this fear, this selfishness – all of these are widespread human characteristics. Therefore, the chances are today, too, people all over the world are left to meet their fate, just like the Frank family.

Even the help of some individuals could not prevent the deportation and extermination of Anne Frank and millions of others.

The Anne Frank Foundation wants to stress in this book that the rejection and prevention of discrimination must start at an early stage and that each of us has a personal responsibility toward achieving this goal. Had these convictions shaped the human consciousness in the 1930s, then the name Hitler would be totally insignificant to us today.

Anne Frank Foundation.

EINLEITUNG

Es gibt Fragen, die wir nicht mehr beantworten können, die sich uns heute aber in anderer Form stellen. Fragen, die uns nicht loslassen.

Hätte Anne Frank, zu Lebzeiten ein Mädchen unter vielen, auf unsere Hilfe rechnen können, wenn sie unser Nachbarskind gewesen wäre? Hätten wir die Gefahren des Faschismus erkannt oder wären wir nicht auch der Propaganda aufgesessen, die weismachen wollte, dass Juden minderwertige Menschen sind?

Vielleicht wären wir damals mit denen einer Meinung gewesen, die die Juden als Verursacher vieler Probleme verurteilten, was sich heute in Grundzügen bei den 'Ausländern' wiederholt.

Ob wir den Mut gehabt hätten, zu widerstehen? Oder hätten wir uns mit einem ohnmächtigen Gefühl in unser Schicksal gefügt?

Viele Deutsche haben sich auf den Nationalsozialismus eingelassen. Doch nicht nur sie, auch Niederländer und Menschen anderer Nationen sind passiv geblieben oder haben sich aktiv beteiligt.

Interesselosigkeit, Angst, Selbstgerechtigkeit und Egoismus sind weltweit verbreitete menschliche Eigenschaften, die dazu führen, dass Menschen wie die Franks im Stich gelassen werden. So konnte es auch geschehen, dass trotz der Hilfe weniger Millionen Menschen, einer von ihnen war Anne, deportiert und vernichtet wurden.

Die Anne Frank Stiftung möchte mit diesem Buch darauf hinweisen, dass die Bekämpfung von Diskriminierung bei frühzeitigem Erkennen und rechtzeitigen vorbeugenden Massnahmen beginnt. Dafür ist jeder Mensch persönlich verantwortlich.

Hätten dies 1930 die Menschen für sich erkannt, würde uns heute der Name Hitler nichts mehr sagen.

Anne Frank Stiftung

TABLE OF CONTENTS

INHALTSANGABE

Ancestors of Anne Frank have lived in Frankfurt since the 17th century. Otto Frank, Anne's father, is born on May 12, 1889, on Frankfurt's *Westend* (West side), a well-to-do neighborhood. His father is a banker. Otto Frank attends high school, and briefly studies art at the University of Heidelberg. Via a friend he is offered and accepts a job from 1908 until 1909 at Macy's Department Store in New York. When his father dies, Otto Frank returns to Germany and works for a metal engineering company in Düsseldorf until 1914. During World War I he and his two brothers serve in the German Army, where Otto attains the rank of lieutenant. After the war he works in his father's bank, but banks are not faring well at that time. While at the bank he becomes acquainted with Edith Holländer, the daughter of a manufacturer. Born in 1900, she grows up in Aachen. Otto and Edith marry in 1925 and settle in Frankfurt. They have two daughters, Margot, born in 1926, and Anne, whose full name is Annelies Marie, born on June 12, 1929.

Die Vorfahren Anne Franks lebten seit dem 17. Jahrhundert in Frankfurt. Der Vater Otto Frank (*1889) wächst im reichen Westend als Sohn eines Bankiers auf. Nach dem Abitur studiert er kurze Zeit Kunst in Heidelberg. Die Jahre 1908 und 1909 verbringt er in Amerika, wo er durch Vermittlung eines Freundes beim grossen Warenhauskonzern 'Macy' arbeiten kann. Als sein Vater im Sterben liegt, kehrt er nach Deutschland zurück. Bis zum Jahre 1914 arbeitet Otto Frank in einem metallverarbeitenden Betrieb in Düsseldorf. Im 1. Weltkrieg dient er zusammen mit zwei Brüdern im Deutschen Heer und wird zum Leutnant befördert. Nach dem Krieg tritt er der Bank seines Vaters bei. Aber für das Bankwesen sind in Deutschland schlechte Zeiten herangebrochen.

In jenen Jahren lernt Otto Frank Edith Holländer kennen. Edith (*1900) stammt aus Aachen und ist die Tochter eines Fabrikanten. 1925 heiraten die beiden und beschliessen, in Frankfurt zu wohnen. 1926 wird Margot geboren, und drei Jahre später folgt Anne, die eigentlich Annelies Marie heisst.

1

2

1 *Family portrait, circa 1900. Front row, Otto Frank in navy suit.*
2 *Otto Frank (right) during World War I, 1916.*
3 *Edith Höllander.*
4 *Edith Holländer and Otto Frank during their honeymoon in San Remo, 1925.*

1 *Sommerfrische der Familie Frank in Wildbad. In der 1.Reihe, im Matrosenanzug, Otto Frank. Um 1900.*
2 *Otto Frank (rechts) als Mitglied eines Lichtmesstrupps im 1. Weltkrieg. Um 1916.*
3 *Edith Frank, geborene Holländer, 1925.*
4 *Hochzeitsreise nach San Remo, 1925.*

4

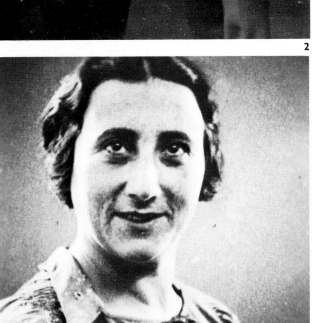

3

2 FRANKFURT AM MAIN IN THE 1920s – PORTRAIT OF A CITY

2 FRANKFURT AM MAIN IN DEN 20ER JAHREN – BILDER EINER STADT

Since the Middle Ages Frankfurt has been an important center of trade and finance. At the end of the 19th century new industrial areas spring up on the east and west side of the city. After annexing surrounding villages, Frankfurt has the largest land area of all German cities at the end of World War I. In 1929 the city has a population of 540,000. The intellectual and political climate is democratic and liberal. The city is governed by a coalition of the social democratic, liberal and christian parties.

Seit dem Mittelalter ist Frankfurt eine wichtige Handels-, Messe- und Bankenstadt. Ende des 19. Jahrhunderts enstehen im Westen und Osten der alten Stadt große Industriegebiete. Nach dem 1. Weltkrieg ist Frankfurt (durch Eingemeindungen) zeitweise die flächenmäßig größte deutsche Stadt. 1929 leben hier 540 000 Menschen. Das geistige und politische Klima ist demokratisch und progressiv. Eine Koalition von Sozialdemokraten, liberalen Demokraten und christlich-katholischen Demokraten regiert die Stadt.

6

5 *Panoramic view of Frankfurt am Main. At left, the Dome, where the German kings and emperors were crowned until 1806.*
6 *St. Paul's Church, site of the first German Parliamentary Assembly in 1848. At right, the monument of Friedrich Ebert, first president of the Weimar Republic.*
7 *The new living quarters offer modern schools, playgrounds and various facilities.*

5 *Ansicht der Frankfurter Altstad von Süden mit dem Dom, bis 1806 Krönungsort der deutschen Kaiser und Könige. Um 1932.*
6 *Die Paulskirche, Ort des ersten deutschen Parlaments 1848; rechts am Turm das Friedrich-Ebert-Denkmal, das die Stadt 1926 anbringen ließ, zum Gedenken an den ersten Präsidenten der Weimarer Republik.*
7 *Die neuen Siedlungen erhielten moderne Schulbauten, Sozialeinrichtungen und Kinderspielplätze. Um 1930.*

5

7

3 FRANKFURT, 1929 – POLITICAL AND ECONOMIC CRISIS

3 FRANKFURT AM MAIN UM 1929 – KRISE VON DEMOKRATIE UND REPUBLIK

The Great Depression of 1929 also causes social and political tension in Frankfurt. Between 1929 and 1932 industrial activity decreases 65%. By the end of 1932, more than 70,000 people are unemployed in Frankfurt. One-fourth of the population – workers and civil servants, in particular – no longer has a steady income. Furthermore, the National Socialists profit from the inability of the democratic system to solve the crisis. The labor movement carries the weight in the political struggle against the threat from the extreme right.

Die Weltwirtschaftskrise, die im Geburtsjahr Anne Franks ausbricht, verschärft auch in Frankfurt die sozialen und politischen Gegensätze. Zwischen 1929 und 1932 schrumpft die industrielle Produktion um 65%. Ende 1932 sind in Frankfurt über 70 000 arbeitslos. 25 % der Einwohner, vor allem Arbeiter und Angestellte, sind ohne gesichertes Einkommen. Auch in Frankfurt profitieren die Nationalsozialisten von der Unfähigkeit der Demokraten, der Krise Herr zu werden. Träger des politischen Kampfes gegen die Bedrohung von rechts ist die Arbeiterbewegung.

8

8

8 In Frankfurt the National Socialists started their organization in the 1920s. The Stahlhelm Day of 1925 is organized by an anti-democratic union comprising former soldiers who fought in World War I.
9 Around 1930 many inhabitants of Frankfurt suffer from poverty. A soup kitchen for the umemployed in the Friedrich Ebert quarter.
10 Anti-Nazi demonstration in Frankfurt organized by the Eiserne Front, an association of several left-wing organizations.

8 Aufmarsch des 'Stahlhelms' in Frankfurt. 1925.
9 Arbeitslosenküche in der Friedrich-Ebert-Siedlung. 1932.
10 Demonstration der 'Eisernen Front' gegen Nationalsozialismus und Faschismus. 1932.

9

10

4 THE JEWISH COMMUNITY OF FRANKFURT

4 JÜDISCHE TRADITION UND KULTUR IN FRANKFURT AM MAIN

In 1929 the number of Jews living in Frankfurt is about 30,000, or roughly 5.5% of the population. It is the second largest Jewish community in Germany (Berlin is first) and dates back to the Middle Ages. At the beginning of the 19th century Jews are no longer required to live in the ghetto, and the law declares them equal. Their new legal status marks the beginning of a process of social and cultural assimilation. Jewish philanthropic organizations play an important role in the development of the city. Although anti-Semitism never fully disappears, Frankfurt is – for the most part – a tolerant city. Jewish citizens are able to maintain their traditional way of life or assimilate into society at large.

1929 leben in der Stadt etwa 30000 Juden, 5½% der Gesamtbevölkerung. Nach Berlin hat Frankfurt die größte jüdische Gemeinde im Reich. Ihre Tradition recht bis in das Mittelalter zurück. Mit der Aufhebung des Ghettos zu Beginn des 19. Jahrhunderts und der rechtlichen Gleichstellung der Juden beginnt ein Prozess der sozialen und kulturellen Assimilation. Reiche jüdische Stiftungen für allgemeine Zwecke bestimmen die Entwicklung der Stadt. Zwar verschwindet der Antisemitismus nie völlig, aber in Frankfurt sind Toleranz und Liberalität vorherrschend, einerlei, ob jüdische Bürger traditionelle Lebensweise und Überzeugungen streng bewahren oder Assimilation und Integration suchen.

11

12

11 *In 1882 a synagogue was built on Börneplatz next to a huge open-air market, 1927.*
12 *The Judengasse (Jews Street) in Frankfurt. When the Jews lived in the ghetto the street was closed every evening, and gentiles were not allowed to enter. Circa, 1872.*
13 *The Kölnerhof Hotel near the Frankfurt Railway Station makes it clear that Jews are unwanted guests, 1905.*

11 *Die 1882 neu erbaute Synagoge am Börneplatz und der Wochenmarkt. 1927.*
12 *Die östliche Häuserseite des Ghettos kurz vor dem Abbruch der Häuser. 1872.*
13 *Antisemitisches Plakat im Hotel 'Kölner Hof' am Hauptbahnhof. 1905.*

13

THE FRANK FAMILY
FRANKFURT, 1929-1933

DIE FAMILIE FRANK
FRANKFURT, 1929-1933

Otto Frank is an enthusiastic amateurphotographer. He takes dozens of photographs of Anne and Margot playing in the street with their friends, visiting their grandparents in Aachen, or going to the countryside.

Otto Frank ist ein begeisteter Hobbyfotograf. Von Anne und Margot hat er viele Fotos gemacht, zuhause, auf der Strasse, mit Freundinnen, bei Kinderfesten, bei den Grosseltern in Aachen und so weiter.

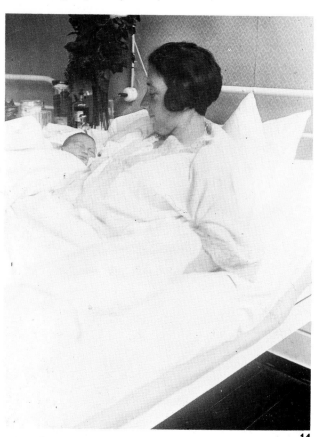

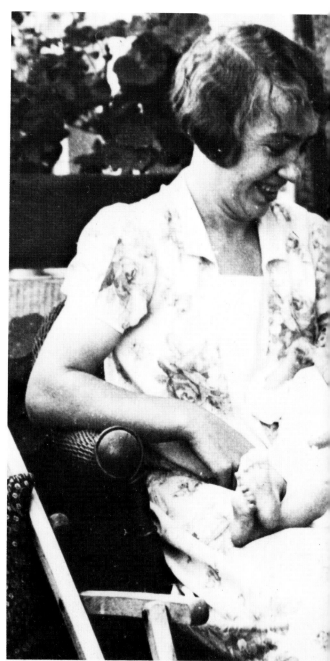

14

14 Anne Frank, one day old, with her mother. June 13, 1929.
15 Margot with her new sister.
16 Margot and Anne.
17 Anne and her mother in Ganghoferstrasse.

14 Anne Frank, einen Tag nach der Geburt, mit ihrer Mutter.
15 Margot mit dem neuen Schwesterchen.
16 Margot und Anne.
17 Anne und ihre Mutter in der Ganghoferstrasse, 1931.

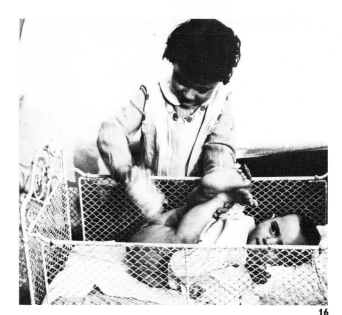

19

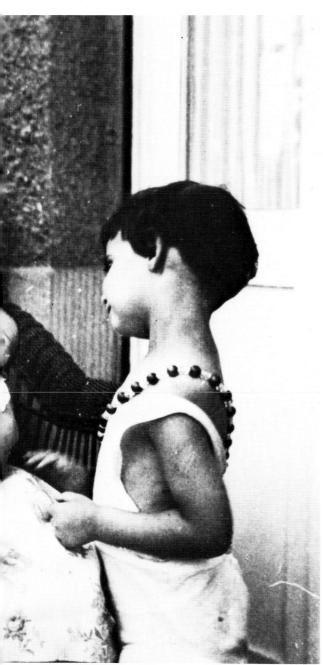

16

17

15

18 *Anne.*
19 *Otto Frank and his two daughters, 1931.*
20 *Anne and Margot.*
21 *Edith Frank with her two daughters near the Hauptwache in Frankfurt's city center.*
22 *Anne, 1932.*

18 *Anne.*
19 *Otto Frank mit seinen Töchtern, 1931.*
20 *Anne und Margot.*
21 *Edith Frank mit ihren Töchtern bei der Hauptwache im Frankfurter Zentrum. 1933.*
22 *Anne, 1932.*

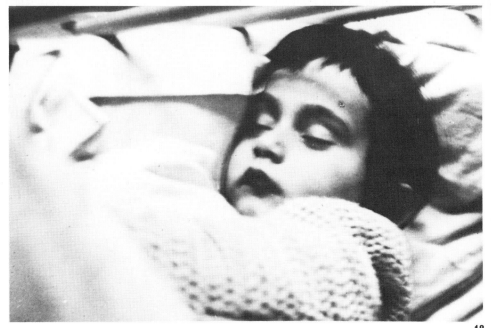

18

19

20

21

22

5,6,7 NATIONAL SOCIALISTS ON THEIR WAY TO POWER

The 1920s and early '30s in Germany are characterized by economic crisis, inflation and hurt pride about the country's defeat during World War I and the subsequent Treaty of Versailles. Workers lose their jobs; farmers, their land; civilians, their savings.

The National Socialist German Workers Party (NSDAP), founded in 1919, recruits more and more followers. Hitler blames not only what he calls the weak government for all problems in Germany but also the Jews.

Fascist movements wanted absolute power, if at all possible through 'democratic' means: in other words, as many votes as possible from the followers. The Nazis shrewdly use the apparent human need for a scapegoat. Just as some political organizations today blame specific groups for all that is wrong, Hitler blamed the Jews.

In January 1933 Hitler wins the elections and becomes the leader of a coalition government partially because the opposition is divided. On March 23, 1933, he seizes absolute power. It is essential that Hitler begins with large popular support. He is able to channel the feelings of uncertainty and discontentment into a mass political movement.

Elsewhere in Europe fascist and National Socialist movements are developing, as well.

Die Weimarer Republik ist gekennzeichnet von Wirtschaftskrise und Inflation. Hinzu kommt bei vielen Deutschen ein infolge des verlorenen Krieges und des Versailler Friedensvertrages verletzter Nationalstolz. Zahlreiche Arbeiter stehen auf der Strasse, Bauern verlieren ihr Land und Sparer ihr Geld. Die 1919 gegründete NSDAP gewinnt immer mehr Anhänger. Hitler gibt den Juden sowie der schwachen Regierung die Schuld an den Schwierigkeiten. Die faschistische Bewegung strebt nach der absoluten Macht – soweit möglich auf demokratischem Weg, d.h. mit Hilfe der Wähler. Geschickt setzt die NSDAP auf das offensichtliche Bedürfnis nach einem Sündenbock. So wie heute einige Parteien 'die Ausländer' als Ursache allen Elends bezeichnen, so bietet Hitler 'die Juden' als Schuldige an. Er gewinnt schliesslich 1933 die Wahlen und tritt trotz fehlender Mehrheit am 30. Januar an die Spitze einer nationalistischen Koalitionsregierung. Das Ermächtigungsgesetz vom 23. März gibt der NSDAP die absolute Staatsmacht.

Festzuhalten ist, dass das NS-Regime mit breiter Volksunterstützung startet. Demagogisch geschickt versteht es Hitler Unzufriedenheit und Verunsicherung in eine starke politische Bewegung umzuleiten. Sein Erfolg lässt überall in Europa ähnliche Bewegungen entstehen.

23 Unemployed Germans. Berlin, 1932.
24 Adolf Hitler (right) as a soldier at the battle front during World War I.
25 Nazi election campaign propaganda.

23 *Arbeitslose in Berlin, 1932.*
24 *Hitler (rechts) als Frontsoldat während des ersten Weltkrieges.*
25 *Wahlkampfzug der NSDAP.*

24

25

26 NSBO, the Nazi trade union, joins in the strikes to gain support.
27 The SA is an attractive alternative for many who are unemployed.
28, 29 The right-wing political parties close ranks and become known as the Harzburger Front. Bad Harzburg, October 1931.

26 Die Nationalsozialistische Betriebsorganisation NSBO beteiligt sich an Streiks, um die Arbeiter für sich zu gewinnen.
27 Die SA ist eine verlockende Alternative zum monotonen Arbeitslosenalltag.
28, 29 Oktober 1931 in Bad Harzburg: Die rechte Opposition verbündet sich (Harzburger Front).

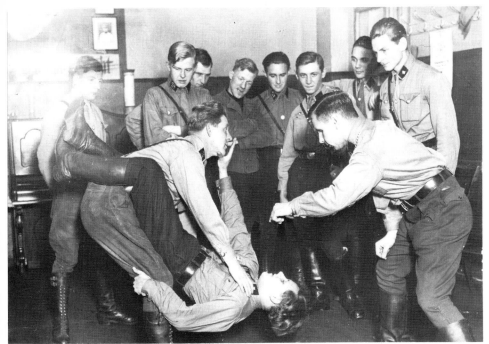

27

28

29

ARBEITER

WÄHLT DEN FRONTSOLDATEN HITLER!

30

33

NATIONAL SOZIALIST

ODER UMSONST WAREN DIE OPFER

Unsere letzte Hoffnung:

HITLER

31

32

30, 31, 32 Nazi posters.
33, 35 As of January 1933 Hitler seizes power. The Nazis celebrate.
34 The Jewish mayor of Frankfurt, Landmann, is replaced by a Nazi, Krebs.
36 The swastika flag at the town hall, Frankfurt, March 1933.

30, 31, 32 Plakate der NSDAP.
33, 35 Machtübernahme am 30. Januar 1933. Die NS feiern ihren Sieg (Hitler, Frick und Göring).
34 Der neue Frankfurter Bürgermeister: der Nationalsozialist Krebs. Der jüdische Bürgermeister Landmann ist seines Amtes enthoben worden.
36 Frankfurt im März 1933. Am Rathaus hängt die Hakenkreuzfahne.

34

35

36

A doctrine of National Socialism is the 'leader principle,' the open rejection of parliamentary democracy. All other political parties are forbidden, and all other political opponents are eliminated.

In 1933 about 150,000 political opponents are sent to concentration camps for 're-education.' In the early years of the Hitler regime elections are organized for the sake of appearance only.

Eines der wesentlichen Merkmale des Nationalsozialismus ist das Führerprinzip und die offene Ablehnung der Demokratie. Das bedeutet das Verbot aller anderen politischen Parteien und die Verfolgung politischer Gegner. Nur der Form halber werden in den ersten Jahren des Hitlerregimes noch Wahlen abgehalten. 1933 verschwinden c.a. 150 000 politische Gegner in Konzentrationslagern zur sogenannten 'Umerziehung'.

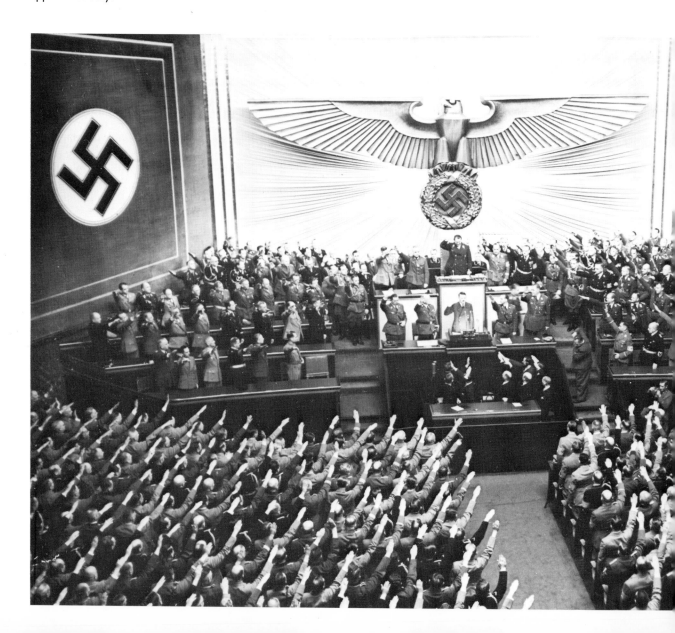

38

37

37 Hitler addresses the Reichstag October 6, 1939.
38 Even deceased democrats are enemies. The monument for Friedrich Ebert, the first president of Germany, is demolished.
39 Oranienburg concentration camp near Berlin. April 6, 1933.

37 Adolf Hitler vor dem Reichstag, 6. Oktober 1939.
38 Auch tote Demokraten sind Staatsfeinde: Am 6. April 1933 wird in Frankfurt das Denkmal zu Ehren des ersten Reichspräsidenten der Weimarer Republik, Friedrich Ebert, gestürzt.
39 Konzentrationslager Oranienburg in der Nähe Berlins, 6. April 1933.

39

On April 1, 1933, Joseph Goebbels declares the official boycott of Jewish shopkeepers, doctors and lawyers.
On April 11, 1933, all public servants with at least one Jewish grandparent are fired. These and scores of other measures are designed to remove Jews from their jobs and businesses. According to the Nazi philosophy, there is only room for pure white German ('Aryans') in the nation. Only Aryans can be 'compatriots' (*Volksgenossen*). Jewish companies are 'Aryanized.' The Nazis force Jewish business owners to sell their property, and the Nazis themselves fire the Jewish personnel.

Goebbels erklärt den 1. April 1933 zum Starttag des öffentlichen Boykotts gegen jüdische Geschäfte, Ärzte und Rechtsanwälte. Am 11. April werden alle Beamten, die mindestens ein jüdisches Grosselternteil haben, aus dem Staatsdienst entfernt. Doch das ist erst der Anfang der antijüdischen Massnahmen. Immer mehr Berufe werden für Juden verboten. Nur 'Arier' gelten als 'Volksgenossen'. Die nationalsozialistische Rassenlehre legt die Kriterien fest. Jüdische Betriebe und Unternehmen werden 'arisiert': die Besitzer enteignet, das jüdische Personal entlassen.

40

42

41

43

44

40, 42, 43 Appeals to boycott Jewish-owned shops.
41 'Jew.' Berlin, 1933.
44 A Jewish shopkeeper wearing his military decorations in front of his store in Cologne.

40, 42, 43 Boykottpropaganda gegen jüdische Geschäfte.
41 Berlin.
44 Ein jüdischer Kaufmann mit seinen Orden aus dem ersten Weltkrieg vor seinem Kölner Geschäft.

45, 46 *Carnival in Cologne. Men dress up as Jews, 1934. 'The last Jews disappear. We're only on a short trip to Lichtenstein or Jaffa.'*
47 *Carnival wagon with men in concentration camp uniforms: 'Away to Dachau.' Nuremberg, 1936.*
48 *At the Nuremberg carnival in 1938. 'National enemies.' A puppet at the gallows wearing a Star of David.*

45

46

47

45, 46 *Karneval in Köln 1934.*
47 *Karnevalszug in Nürnberg 1936.*
48 *Karneval in Nürnberg 1938:*
Wagen mit dem Motto
'Volksschädlinge'.

48

34

The Nazis try very quickly to dispand the labor movement. The arrest of 10,000 active members in March 1933 is a heavy blow to the trade unions. In spite of terror and repression, anti-Nazi trade union groups get 80% of the vote during company elections that same month.

On May 1, 1933, Hitler announces the celebration of the 'Day of National Labor.' The largest trade union, ADGB, calls on its members to participate. However, it turns into a mass Nazi manifestation. On May 2 the Nazis occupy the trade union buildings and seize union property. Trade union leaders are replaced by Nazis. The DAF (German Workers Front) is the only union allowed to operate as of May 10, 1933. All workers are forced to become members. There is no place for an independent labor movement that protects the interests of its members. Workers and employers must cooperate. Strikes are forbidden.

Die Arbeiterbewegung ist eines der ersten Angriffsziele der Nazis. Die Verhaftung von 10000 aktiven Mitgliedern im März 1933 trifft die Gewerkschaftsbewegung sehr schwer. Doch trotz des NS-Terrors erringen die freien bewerkschaften bei den Betriebsratswahlen 80% der Stimmen. Obwohl Hitler den 1. Mai zum 'Tag der nationalen Arbeit' ausruft, fordert der Allgemeine Deutsche Gewerkschaftsbund, ADGB, zur Teilnahme auf, in der Hoffnung, dass der Feiertag der Arbeiterbewegung zu einer Antinazidemonstration wird. Doch die Regie führen die Nazis. Entgegen den Intentionen des ADGB wird der Tag zu einer gigantischen NS-Manifestation. Schon am folgenden Tag besetzen die Nationalsozialisten die Gewerkschaftsgebäude und beschlagnahmen ihr Eigentum. Am 10. Mai wird die 'Deutsche Arbeitsfront' als Pflichtverband für alle Arbeiter gegründet. Das ist das Ende der freien Gewerkschaftsbewegung.

50

51

49 Communists and Social
Democrats are arrested by the SA.
Spring 1933.
50 Throughout Germany millions of
people celebrate the Day of
National Labor on May 1, 1933.
Munich.
51 On May 2, 1933, the SA seizes
the trade union buildings
throughout the entire country.
Berlin.

49 Frühjahr 1933. Zahlreiche
Kommunisten und
Sozialdemokraten werden von
SA-Einheiten verhaftet. Die SA tritt
als Hilfspolizei auf.
50 1. Mai 1933, München: Hitlers
'Tag der nationalen Arbeit' zieht in
ganz Deutschland Millionen
Teilnehmer an.
51 Am 2. Mai 1933: Die SA besetzt
in vielen Städten die
Gewerkschaftshäuser. Berlin.

12 THE LABOR SERVICE

12 DER ARBEITSDIENST

To fight the vast unemployment, the Nazis initiate employment projects: construction of freeways (*Autobahnen*) and fortification of the arms industry. The country's economy changes to a war economy. To that end everyone must contribute. Teen-agers and young adults are forced to work an allotted period of time for a nominal fee. Simultaneously, they are indoctrinated in Nazi ideology. From 1938 on workers in certain professions are forced to work in the war industry.

Gegen die grosse Arbeitslosigkeit setzen die Nazis Arbeitsbeschaffungsprogramme: zum Beispiel den Autobahnbau oder Kriegsgüterproduktion. Im Januar 1933 wird der Arbeitsdienst für alle Jugendlichen zur gesetzlichen Pflicht. Gegen minimales Entgelt wird schwere Arbeit verlangt und nationalsozialistische Indoktrination geboten. Am 1938 kommt es in der Kriegsindustrie zu Arbeitsdienstverpflichtungen von Fachkräften.

52 On behalf of 40,000 male and 2,000 female labor service workers, their leader pledges allegiance to Hitler. September 1938.
53 Workers marching to work.
54 Handing out of shovels to build the freeways.

52 September 1938. In Namen von 40 000 Arbeitern und 2000 Arbeiterinnen schwört Reichsarbeitsleiter Hierl Hitler die Treue.
53 Kollonenweise marschieren die Arbeiter zur Baustelle.
54 Schaufeln für den Autobahnbau werden verteilt. Frankfurt, 23. September 1933.

53

54

13 THE NATIONAL SOCIALIST 'WELFARE STATE'

13 DER VÖLKISCHE 'VERSORGUNGSSTAAT'

The Nazi state gives the impression it is taking care of everything: vacations, recreation, art and culture, health care for mother and child, etc. This, however, applies only to those who are 'Volksgenossen': racially 'pure' and mentally and physically healthy.

The Nazis believe that a healthy nation should not spend money on the mentally handicapped. Consequently, thousands of mentally handicapped are quietly killed beginning in 1939. In contrast to their silence about the Jews, the churches voice indignation and protest over the killing of the mentally handicapped. The so-called euthanasia project is stopped in 1941. A total of 72,000 physically and mentally handicapped men, women and children and alcoholics are killed by injection or gas. In the last years of the Hitler regime another 130,000 patients die of starvation or cold.

Der NS-Staat vereinnahmt alle gesellschaftlichen Bereiche. Er kümmert sich um Freizeit und Ferien, Kunst und Kultur, Gesundheit für Mutter und Kind, verspricht jeder deutschen Familie ein Auto. In den Genuss dieser Vergünstigungen sollen allerdings nur reinrassige, körperlich und geistig gesunde Volksgenossen kommen. Überzeugung des NS-Staates: die Versorgung Behinderter kostet zuviel Geld und ist für ein gesundes Volk ein überflüssiger Luxus. Ab 1939 beginnt man im Geheimen tausende von geistig und körperlich Behinderten umzubringen. Als die Kirchen davon erfahren, kommt es erstmals zu öffentlichen Protesten von den Kanzeln. 1941 wird das sogenannte 'Euthanasieprojekt' eingestellt. Bis zu diesem Zeitpunkt haben die Nazis bereits 72 000 Menschen durch Injektionen und Vergasung umgebracht: geistig und körperlich Behinderte, Drogen- und Alkoholabhängige.

56

58

57

59

55, 56, 57 *The Kraft Durch Freude (Strength Through Joy) organization promises vacations and entertainment for every German: a trip to Madeira or Libya, to the mountains to ski or to the beach to swim. Even the famous Fratellini clowns perform for Kraft Durch Freude in the Horst Wessel Hospital. Kraft Durch Freude organizes vacations for one million Germans.*

58, 59 *With comparisons like these, the Nazis try to influence public opinion. 'A genetically healthy family is forced to live in an old railroad car.' 'Hereditarily mentally handicapped people in an institution.' From 'Little Handbook for Heredity and Race Sciences,' 1934.*

55, 56, 57 *'Des Führers Werk hat es ermöglicht'. Die Freizeitorganisation der Deutschen Arbeitsfront 'Kraft durch Freude' verspricht allen Deutschen Urlaub und Entspannung: eine Reise nach Madeira oder in die lybische Wüste. Geboten werden Wintersport wie Strandferien. Selbst die weltberühmten Clowns 'Die Fratelinis' treten für 'Kraft durch Freude' im Berliner Horst-Wessel-Krankenhaus auf. Eine Million Deutsche machen auf diese Weise erstmals Urlaub.*

58, 59 *'Erbgesunde deutsche Familie, die in einem alten Eisenbahnwagen leben muss'. 'Erbkranke (Schwachsinnige) in einer Heilanstalt'.*

40

The Nazis encourage large families. More children mean more future soldiers. But these children must be racially 'pure' and healthy. On July 14, 1933, a law is introduced 'to prevent genetically unfit offspring.' The result: forced sterilization for individuals who are mentally handicapped, epileptic, deaf or blind.

1935: the Nuremberg laws 'protect German blood and German honor' by forbidding marriage between Jews and Aryans and by punishing Jews and Aryans who engage in sexuall intercourse.

1937: the Gestapo (Nazi police) brings 385 black German children to university hospitals to be sterilized.

Die Nazis fördern kinderreiche Familien: je mehr Kinder, desto mehr Soldaten. Aber die Kinder müssen hundertprozentig gesund sowie 'rassenrein' sein. Um dies sicherzustellen, wird am 14. Juli 1933 das 'Gesetz zur Verhütung erbkranken Nachwuchses' in Kraft gesetzt. Zur Pflicht werden u.a. die Sterilisation bei erblicher Geisteskrankheit, Epilepsie; Taub- und Blindheit. 1935 folgen die Nürnberger Gesetze 'Zum Schutze des deutschen Blutes und der deutschen Ehre'. Sie verbieten Ehen zwischen 'Ariern' und Juden und stellen Geschlechtsverkehr zwischen ihnen unter Strafe. 1937: Die Gestapo bringt 385 schwarze deutsche Kinder zur Sterilisation in Universitätskliniken.

60

62

61

63

60, 61, 62, 63 'This is how a German mother looks, and this is a non-German alien mother. These are children of your own blood, and these belong to an alien race.' From the SS booklet 'Victory of Arms, Victory of Children.'
64 Day of Large Families. Frankfurt, 1937.

60, 61, 62, 63 'So sieht eine deutsche Mutter aus, und so eine artfremde'. 'Das sind Kinder Euren Blutes, und jene gehören einer fremden Rasse an'.
64 Frankfurt 1937: Der Reichstag der Kinderreichen.

42

Beginning in 1933 only one youth movement is allowed: the Hitler Youth (*Hitler Jugend*). All other organizations are either incorporated or forbidden. The aim is to convert youth into National Socialists. For boys the emphasis is on military training; for girls, motherhood.
The youth movement focuses on sports and physical activities. Reading and learning are of secondary importance.

Ab 1933 gibt es in Deutschland nur noch eine einzige offizielle Jugendorganisation: die Hitlerjugend. Alle anderen sind entweder in ihr aufgegangen oder verboten. Das Ziel ist es, die Jugendlichen zu wahren Nationalsozialisten zu formen. Bei den Jungen überwiegt das militärische Training. Die Mädchen werden auf die Mutterschaft vorbereitet. Schwerpunkte der Hitlerjugend sind Sport und körperliche Bewegung. Auf Lesen und Lernen wird wenig Wert gelegt.

66

65 Not all members of Hitlerjugend (Hitler Youth) have a uniform by 1933.
66, 67 The Hitler Youth and the Bund Deutscher Mädel (League of German Girls) offer a variety of leisure activities.
68 Children between the ages of 10 to 14 are organized in the Jungvolk (Young Folk).

65 Hitlerjugend 1933. Noch sind nicht alle uniformiert.
66, 67 Die Hitlerjugend sowie der Bund Deutscher Mädel, der BDM, organisieren attraktive Freizeitgestaltung.
68 Kinder von 10–14 werden zum 'Jungvolk' angemustert.

67

65

68

17 EDUCATION

Education becomes National Socialist-oriented.

44 In April 1933 a law is passed to fire all teachers who are Jews or political opponents. Hundreds of textbooks are replaced by Nazi-written material. New subjects, such as genetics and the study of race and nation, are introduced.

The universities replace professors. Political opponents and Jews are stripped of their academic titles. The number of Jewish and female students is limited.

In 1938 Jews are barred from schools and universities altogether.

Im NS-Staat wird das gesamte Bildungssystem an der Nazi-Ideologie ausgerichtet. Schon im April 1933 wird ein Gesetz erlassen, durch das alle politischen Gegner sowie die Juden aus dem Schuldienst entfernt werden. Schulbücher werden durch nationalsozialistisches Lehrmaterial ersetzt. Neue Pflichtfächer werden eingeführt wie Erblichkeitslehre, Rassen- und Völkerkunde. Auch die Hochschulen und Universitäten werden von Gegnern und Juden gesäubert. Die Zahl der jüdischen und weiblichen Studenten wird begrenzt. Ab 1938 ist Juden der Besuch von Schulen und Hochschulen gänzlich verboten.

70

69 Schoolchildren learn the Hitler salute.
70 Eugen Fischer, chancellor of the Univerisity of Berlin, is replaced by Wilhelm Krüger, who wears the traditional robe over his SS uniform, 1935.
71 Die Weisse Rose (The White Rose) is a student resistance organization in Munich, 1942. Hans and Sophie Scholl, brother and sister, are active members. They are caught by the Gestapo and executed after a quick trial. Anti-Nazi student groups such as these spring up in various German university towns.

69 Früh übt sich, was ein Meister werden will: Schulkinder.
70 Rektorenwechsel an der Friedrich-Wilhelm-Universität Berlin, April 1935. Nachfolger von Eugen Fischer wird Wilhelm Krüger. Unter der Amtsrobe stellt er ganz offen seine SS-Uniform zur Schau.
71 München 1942. Die studentische Widerstandsgruppe 'Weisse Rose', initiert von Hans Scholl, verteilt Flugblätter gegen das NS-Regime. Die Gestapo spürt sie auf, verhaftet ihre Mitglieder. Im Schnellverfahren werden die Geschwister Scholl und ihre Mitkämpfer zum Tode verurteilt, anschliessend hingerichtet. Auch in anderen Universitätsstädten bilden sich ähnliche Widerstandsgruppen.

71

46

Nazism is dependent upon propaganda. Mass meetings, photos, posters, stamps – they all are used to propagate the Nazi ideology. Nazis consider propaganda so important they even create a special Ministry of Propaganda under the leadership of Goebbels.

Der Nationalsozialismus lebt von der Propaganda. Massenversammlungen, Fotos, Plakate: alles dient allein ein- und demselben Ziel: der Verbreitung des nationalsozialistischen Gedankengutes. Das Reichspropagandaministerium unter Joseph Goebbels übernimmt Leitung, Lenkung und Koordination.

72 *A swastika flag for every household.*
73 *The annual 'Day of the Party, a gigantic propaganda meeting. 1937.*
74 *Propaganda from the magazine, stürmer: 'The Jews Are Our Misfortune.'*

72 *Für jede deutsche Familie eine Hakenkreuzfahne.*
73 *Die jährlichen 'Reichsparteitage' in Nürnberg sind gigantische Propagandakundgebungen.*
74 *'Stürmer'-Werbekasten Gaubereich Worms.*

73

74

48

In Hilter's Germany art and culture are made totally subordinate to the Nazi ideology. All works of art by Jews and political opponents are destroyed or confiscated and henceforth forbidden.
The independent artist can no longer work. Painters, musicians and authors are forced to join Goebbels' 'chamber of culture' in order to continue working.

Das gesamte Kulturleben wird im Dritten Reich der Naziideologie unterworfen und gleichgeschaltet. Werke jüdischer und politisch unliebsamer Künstler werden verboten, vernichtet oder beschlagnahmt. Die freie Berufswahl wird dadurch aufgehoben, daß fortan jeder Künstler der neu gegründeten 'Reichskulturkammer' beitreten muß. Nichtmitgliedern wird jegliche künstlerische Betätigung verboten.

75

75 Artists are forced to choose between leaving the country or adapting to the new situation. Film director Leni Riefenstahl (center) puts her skills to use for the Nazis. Her famous propaganda movie is 'Triumph des Willens' (Victory of the Will), a documentary of the Nazi Party Day in Nuremberg.
76, 77, 78 The burning of banned books in Berlin. May 1933.

75 Künstlern bleibt nur die Wahl zwischen Emigration oder Anpassung, bzw. Berufsaufgabe. Die Filmregisseurin Leni Riefenstahl stellt sich völlig in den Dienst des NS-Regimes. Ihre bekannteste Arbeit: der Propagandafilm 'Triumph des Willens', gedreht auf dem NSDAP-Parteitag 1935.
76, 77, 78 Bücherverbrennungen Mai 1933.

76

77

78

50

Although the Nazi ideology is basically anti-Christian, from 1933 on the Nazis can count on ample support from the German churches. With few exceptions both the Protestant and Catholic churches endorse the racial and political principles of the Nazis.

On March 28, 1933, the Catholic bishops declare their loyalty to Hitler. The next month the Protestant *Altpreussische Union* also endorses Hitler.

During elections in the Evangelical Church on July 25, 1933, the anti-Semitic 'German Christians' capture a large majority. The official churches fail to protest against the persecution of the Jews, even Jews who had converted to Christianity.

Obwohl die Nazi-Ideologie im Grunde genommen antichristlich ist, erfreuen sich die Nazis dennoch seit 1933 breiter Unterstützung der deutschen Kirchen. Bis auf wenige Ausnahmen stehen sowohl die katholischen als auch die protestantischen Kirchen hinter den Staats- und Rassenlehren. Schon am 28. März erklären die katholischen Bischöfe Hitler gegenüber ihre Treue. Bei den Wahlen innerhalb der evangelischen Kirche am 25. Juli 1933 erreichen die antisemitischen 'Deutschen Christen' eine große Mehrheit. Von offiziellen Kirchenstellen beider Glaubensgemeinschaften hört man kein Wort des Protestes gegen die Judenverfolgung. Selbst getaufte Juden werden im Stich gelassen.

79 Bishop Müller. September 25, 1934.
80 Meeting of the Deutsche Christen (German Christians) in the Berlin Sports Palace. November 13, 1934.
81 Hildegard Schaeder is a member of the Bekennende Kirche to which Dietrich Bonhoeffer and Martin Niemöller also belong. Unlike the official churches, this group protests from the very beginning against the persecution of the Jews. Mrs. Schaeder helps refugees and Jews leave Germany. Between 1943 and 1945 she is detained in Ravensbrück concentration camp.

80

79 Reichsbischof Müller im Lustgarten Berlin, 25. September 1934.
80 Versammlung der 'Deutschen Christen' im Berliner Sportpalast.
81 Trotz der Zusammenarbeit zwischen Nazis und Kirchenführung gibt es auch in den Kirchen Widerstand gegen das NS-Regime. Er manifestiert sich u.a. in der 'Bekennenden Kirche', die gegen die Judenverfolgung protestiert. Zu ihren bekanntesten Mitgliedern gehören Martin Niemöller und Dietrich Bonhoeffer. Hildegard Schaeder versorgt Juden und hilft ihnen bei der Flucht. Dafür stecken sie die Nazis von 1943 bis 1945 in das KZ Ravensbrück.

81

Shortly after seizing power, Hitler meets with the top echelon of the German Army to propose his plans. The 'Shame of Versailles' must be erased. Rearmament, return of the lost territories and new 'space to live' (*Lebensraum*) in the east are his goals. The army is willing on one condition: that the power of the SA, Hitler's paramilitary organization consisting of 2.5 million men, is limited.
On Hitler's orders, the top leaders of the SA are murdered on June 30, 1934.
At the end of 1934 the army swears its oath of loyalty to Hitler personally. In 1935 the draft is introduced.

Wenige Tage nach der Machtübernahme trifft Hitler mit der Heeresleitung zusammen, um seine militärischen Pläne bekanntzugeben. An erster Stelle steht dabei die Wiederaufrüstung Deutschlands sowie die Zurückeroberung der damals verlorenen Gebiete. Zusätzlich soll 'Lebensraum' im Osten gewonnen werden. Die Heeresleitung stimmt zu unter der Voraussetzung, daß Hitler die Macht der paramilitärischen SA, eines lästigen Konkurrenten, beschneidet. Auf Führerbefehl hin wird am 30. Juni 1934 die gesamte SA-Leitung von der SS liquidiert. 1935 wird die allgemeine Wehrpflicht wiedereingeführt.

82 *General Ludwig Beck resigns in 1938 after learning of Hitler's plan to attack Czechoslovakia. Later, Beck is involved in the attempted murder of Hitler on July 20, 1944. When the attack fails, he commits suicide.*
83 *The first group of new recruits. June, 1935.*
84 *The arms industry in full action. Between 1934 and 1939 more than 60 billion German Marks are spent on armament.*

82 *Generaloberst Ludwig Beck tritt 1938 aus Protest gegen die Angriffspläne gegen die Tschechoslowakei zurück. Später beteiligt er sich am mißglückten Attentat auf Hitler am 20. Juli 1944, wird verhaftet und zum Selbstmord getrieben.*
83 *Der erste Jahrgang neuer Rekruten, Juni 1935.*
84 *Die Rüstungsindustrie arbeitet auf Hochtouren. Zwischen 1934 und 1939 werden rund 60 Milliarden Reichsmark in die Rüstung gesteckt. Gleichzeitig sinken die Sozialausgaben. Insgesamt werden hierfür zwischen 1934 und 1938 4 Mrd. Reichsmark aufgewendet.*

82

83

84

54

In April 1933 Adolf Hitler receives a delegation of German judges. Although the judges dedicate themselves to the new order, they ask that in return for their loyalty, Hitler agree to guarantee their independence. Hitler does agree, provided certain 'necessary measures' are taken.

The delegation approves his measures, and as a result, Jews and political opponents are fired.

A few judges realize the ramifications and retire. Other judges believe that by staying on, worse situations can be prevented. Soon, however, the judicial system becomes part of the terror machinery. To begin with, the judges accept the race laws and evidence obtained by torture. Then they accept the unrestricted actions of the SA, SS and Gestapo against so-called traitors. And finally, they even accept that Jews, homosexuals and gypsies are being stripped of any rights.

Am 7. April 1933 empfängt Hitler eine Delegation der deutschen Richterschaft. Sie bieten ihm ihre Unterstützung an, bitten jedoch um eine Bestätigung der richterlichen Unabhängigkeit. Hitler gewährt diese unter bestimmten Voraussetzungen: Entfernung der Juden sowie aller politischer Gegner aus dem Justizapperat. Die Säuberung der Justiz stößt kaum auf Widerstand. Nur wenige Richter legen ihr Amt aus Protest nieder. Viele bleiben in der Überzeugung, so Schlimmeres verhüten zu können. Der Rest sind überzeugte Nazis.

Binnen kurzer Zeit sind Rechtspflege und -apparat in das System des Terrors eingegliedert. Die Justiz akzeptiert die Rassengesetze. Durch Folter erzwungene Geständnisse gelten als Beweismittel. Die Selbstjustiz durch SA, SS und Gestapo wird schweigend toleriert. Widerstandslos wird hingenommen, daß bestimmte Bevölkerungsgruppen wie Juden, Zigeuner oder Homosexuelle völlig entrechtet werden.

85 *Street control in Berlin, 1933.*
86 *A member of the SA (right) serves as a police officer. The original caption of this photo read: 'Law and order restored in the streets of Berlin.'*
87 *The SA in action. Their victims have no rights.*
88 *The SA and SS (Schutz Staffel, an elite military corps that protects party officials) Nazi troops are incorporated into the German police force in March 1933.*

85 *Straßenkontrolle Berlin, 1933.*
86 *Ein SA-Man als Polizist.*
87 *Die SA in Aktion.*
88 *SA und SS werden zur offiziellen Hilfspolizei. Potsdam 1933, Vereidigung von SS-Männern.*

86

87

88

56

Between November 9 and 11, 1938, scores of synagogues and thousands of Jewish-owned shops are ransacked and burned. This is known as 'Crystal Night,' named after the shattered glass windows which were a result of the rampage. The Crystal Night signifies an important, stepped-up persecution of the Jews.
Starting November 12 the first mass arrests of Jews take place. About 30,000 Jewish men and boys are taken and deported to the Buchenwald, Dachau and Sachsenhausen concentration camps.

Zwischen dem 9. und 11. November 1938 werden von NS-Leuten dutzende Synagogen sowie tausender jüdischer Läden und Gebäude verwüstet und in Brand gesteckt. Die Judenverfolgung wird von nun an stark forciert. In den folgenden Tagen kommt es zu massenhaften Festnahmen jüdischer Bürger. Rund 30000 Jungen und Männer werden in die Konzentrationslager Buchenwald, Dachau und Sachsenhausen verschleppt.

89 *Jewish shops with shattered windows.*
90 *Frankfurt's synagogue afire, November 9, 1938.*
91, 92 *The ruins of a synagogue in Oranienburger Street, Berlin.*

89 *Jüdischer Läden nach der 'Kristallnacht'.*
90 *Börneplatz, 9. November 1938. Die Frankfurter Synagoge geht in Flammen auf.*
91, 92 *Ruine der Berliner Synagoge in der Oranienburgerstraße.*

90

91

92

58

From 1933 on more and more Jews leave Germany but *Kristallnacht* in 1938 triggers a mass exodus. By the spring of 1939 about half of Germany's 500,000 Jews have left. The problem for Jews is where to go.

Jewish refugees are not welcome everywhere. Many countries quickly place a quota on the number of Jews they allow to enter, or in some cases, countries even close their borders to Jews. As a result, German-Jewish refugees are scattered throughout the world, sometimes through bizarre and round-about ways.

Ab 1933 entschließen sich immer mehr Juden dazu, Deutschland zu verlassen. Im Laufe des Jahres 1938, insbesondere nach der 'Reichskristallnacht', steigt der Strom jüdischer Flüchtlinge stark an. Im Frühjahr 1939 hat rund die Hälfte der etwa 500 000 deutschen Juden das Reich verlassen. Sie sind keineswegs überall willkommen. Schon frühzeitig beschränken viele Länder den Zuzug jüdischer Emigranten. Bisweilen werden die Grenzen sogar ganz geschlossen. So kommt es, daß die deutschen Juden über die ganze Welt verstreut werden.

93

93

93 *A travel agency on Meineke Street. Berlin, 1939.*
94, 95 *Jewish refugees on their way to England.*
96 *Arrival of Jewish refugees in Shanghai. By 1940 about 20,000 are allowed to settle there.*

93 *Reisebüro in der Meinekestraße, Berlin 1939.*
94, 95 *Jüdische Flüchtlinge auf dem Weg nach England.*
96 *Ankunft in Shanghai. 1940 dürfen 20 000 Juden einreisen.*

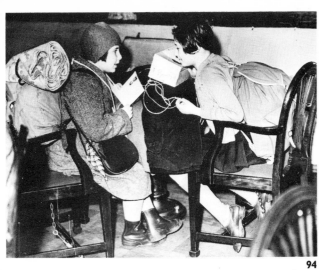

94

95

96

60

March 7, 1936	Germany occupies the demilitarized Rhineland.
March 12, 1938	Austria's annexation.
September 29, 1938	The Munich Treaty. France and Great Britain agree to the occupation of Sudetenland.
August 23, 1939	Nonaggression pact between Germany and the Soviet Union; Poland is divided between them.
September 1, 1939	Germany invades Poland.
September 3, 1939	France and Great Britain declare war on Germany.
April 9, 1940	Germany invades Denmark and Norway.
May 10, 1940	Germany invades Holland, Belgium, Luxembourg and France.
August 27, 1940	Germany, Italy and Japan form a pact.
September 12, 1940	Germany invades Romania.
April 6, 1941	Germany invades Yugoslavia and Greece.
December 7, 1941	Japan attacks Pearl Harbor.
December 8, 1941	The United States declares war on Japan.
December 11, 1941	Germany and Italy declare war on the United States.
November 7, 1942	American and British troops land in North Africa.
February 2, 1943	The German 6th Army capitulates at Stalingrad.
July 10, 1943	Allied landing in Sicily.
June 4, 1944	Liberation of Rome.
June 6, 1944	Allied invasion in Normandy France (D-Day).
June 22, 1944	Russian advance on the Eastern Front.
July 20, 1944	Lt. Col. von Stauffenberg perpetrates a bomb attack against Hitler. The attack fails.
September 11, 1944	American soldiers reach the border of Germany.
February 4, 1945	Conference in Yalta. The United States, Great Britain and the Soviet Union discuss the division of spheres of influence in Europe.
May 5, 1945	Liberation of Holland.
May 8, 1945	The German Army surrenders unconditionally.
August 6, 1945	Atomic bombs on Hiroshima and Nagasaki force Japan to surrender.

25 POLITISCHE UND MILITÄRISCHE EREIGNISSE

7. März, 1936	Deutschland besetzt das entmilitarisierte Rheinland.
12. März, 1938	Österreich wird dem deutschen Reich angeschlossen.
29. September, 1938	Der Münchener Vertrag. Frankreich und England sind damit einverstanden, dass Deutschland das Sudetenland besetzt, einen Teil der Tschechoslowakei.
23. August, 1939	Nichtangriffspakt zwischen Deutschland und der Sowjetunion. Polen wird zwischen beiden Parteien aufgeteilt.
1. September, 1939	Deutschland marschiert in Polen ein.
3. September, 1939	Frankreich und England erklären Deutschland den Krieg.
9. April, 1940	Deutschland marschiert in Dänemark und Norwegen ein.
10. Mai, 1940	Deutschland überfällt die Niederlande, Belgien, Luxemburg und Frankreich.
27. August, 1940	Deutschland, Italien und Japan schliessen sich zusammen.
12. September, 1940	Deutsche Truppen in Rumänien.
6. April, 1941	Deutsche Truppen fallen in Griechenland und Jugoslawien ein.
7. Dezember, 1941	Japan greift die amerikanische Basis Pearl Harbour an.
8. Dezember, 1941	Die USA erklären Japan den Krieg.
11. Dezember, 1941	Deutschland und Italien erklären den USA den Krieg.
7. Dezember, 1942	Amerikanische und englische Truppen landen in Nordafrika.
2. Februar, 1943	Die 6.Armee kapituliert bei Stalingrad.
10. Juli, 1943	Die Alliierten landen auf Sizilien.
4. Juli, 1944	Rom wird befreit.
6. Juni, 1944	Invasion der Alliierten in der Normandie (D-Day).
22. Juni, 1944	Sowjetische Gegenoffensive führt zum Zusammenbruch der Ostfront.
20. Juli, 1944	Oberst von Stauffenberg verübt einen Bombenanschlag auf Hitler, der jedoch mißlingt.
11. September, 1944	Die amerikanischen Truppen erreichen die deutsche Grenze.
4. Februar, 1945	Die Konferenz zu Jalta. Die Sowjetunion, England und die USA teilen Europa in politische Machtsphären auf.
5. Mai, 1945	Niederlande befreit.
8. Mai, 1945	Bedingungslose Kapitulation des deutschen Heeres.
6. August, 1945	Die Atombomben auf Hiroshima und Nagasaki zwingen Japan zur Kapitulation. – der 2. Weltkrieg ist zu Ende.

26 JEWISH LIFE IN HOLLAND BEFORE 1940

The Jewish population in Holland in 1940 is about 140,000, 24,000 of whom are refugees. The Dutch government, which is not convinced of the Jews' need to flee from Germany, restricts the number of immigrants allowed into Holland. The only assistance available to refugees is in camps like Westerbork, for which the Dutch Jewish community is required to pay all costs.

Amsterdam has the largest Jewish community: 90,000. Most are poor. They work in the trade, garment and diamond industries.

Although there are expressions of anti-Semitism, most Jews feel they have assimilated into the Dutch community.

26 DIE JÜDISCHE GEMEINSCHAFT IN DEN NIEDERLANDEN VOR DEM KRIEG

1940 zählen die Niederlande 140 000 jüdische Einwohner, darunter 24 000 Flüchtlinge. Die Regierung verfolgt eine sehr strikte Flüchtlingspolitik, da sie von der Notwendigkeit zur Flucht aus dem Deutschen Reich nicht überzeugt ist. Die Hilfeleistungen beschränken sich auf Auffanglager wie das Barackenlager Westerbork. Die Kosten hat die jüdische Gemeinde zu tragen.

Amsterdam hat bei weitem die größte jüdische Gemeinde: rund 90 000 Menschen. Die meisten sind arm. Viele arbeiten im Handel oder in der Diamanten- und Bekleidungsindustrie. Trotz antisemitischer Äußerungen empfindet sich die große Mehrheit der jüdischen Gemeinschaft als integraler Teil der niederländischen Gesellschaft.

97

97 Uilenburg, a street in the Jewish quarter in Amsterdam.
98 Matzo bakery in the Jewish quarter in Amsterdam.
99 The Waterloo Square market located in the center of the Jewish quarter, Amsterdam.
100 Jews at work in the diamond industry.

97 Im Amsterdamer Judenviertel: Uilenburg.
98 Matze-Bäcker im Amsterdamer Judenviertel.
99 Der Waterloopleinmarkt in Amsterdam mitten im Jüdischen Viertel.
100 In den Diamantschleifereien arbeiten viele Juden.

98

99

100

THE FRANK FAMILY
HOLLAND, 1933-1940.

DIE FAMILIE FRANK
DIE NIEDERLANDE 1933-1940

In 1933, after Hitler seizes power and the anti-Jewish boycott, Otto Frank leaves Frankfurt for Amsterdam. He starts a branch of the German Opekta Co. there, and soon Edith, Margot and Anne join him.

The Frank family moves into a house on Merwedeplein in the southern part of the city. Anne and Margot attend the Montessori School nearby. They have lots of friends, and photographs are proof of the many excursions they took. The Franks become good friends with some other Jewish emigrants who settle in the same neighborhood. The Opekta Co. is doing rather well.

However, this apparent carefree life is suddenly interrupted by the German invasion in May 1940.

1933 – Hitler übernimmt die Macht – verlässt Otto Frank Deutschland und geht nach Amsterdam. Hier eröffnet er eine Filiale der deutschen Firma Opekta. Schon bald folgen ihm Edith, Margot und Anne in die Niederlande.

Die Familie findet in Amsterdam-Süd, am Merwedeplein, eine Wohnung. Hier werden Anne und Margot aufwachsen.

Sie gehen beide auf die in der Nähe gelegene Montessori-Schule, haben viele Freundinnen und machen oft Ausflüge. In diesem Viertel wohnen zu dieser Zeit viele jüdische Emigranten, und mit einigen freundet sich die Familie Frank gut an. Die Geschäfte der Firma Opekta laufen verhältnismässig gut. Doch der deutsche Einmarsch im Mai 1940 macht dem ziemlich ungestörten Leben ein Ende.

101

102

101, 102 *Anne with her girl friend Sanne on Merwedeplein, Amsterdam.*
103, 104 *Summer 1934.*
105 *Anne with a girl friend, 1934.*

101, 102 *Anne mit ihrer Freundin, Sanne, auf dem Merwedeplein in Amsterdam.*
103, 104 *Sommer 1934.*
105 *Anne mit einer Freundin, 1934*

103

104

105

106

106 Anne attends a Montessori
school, 1936.
107 In Amstelrust Park with a
rabbit, 1938.

106 Anne auf der Montessori-
Schule, 1936.
107 Im Amstelrust Park mit einem
Kaninchen.

108 Anne's 10th birthday. June 12,
1939 (Anne, second from left).
109 Anne.
110 Margot, a girl friend and Anne
on the beach at Middelkerke,
Belgium. July 1937.

108 Annes 10. Geburtstag (2.v.l.).
109 Anne.
110 Margot, eine Freundin und
Anne am Strand in Middelkerke,
Belgien, Juli 1937.

108

109

110

111

112

111 *Anne on the roof of the house on
Merwedeplein, 1940.*
112 *The Frank family on
Merwedeplein, May 1940.*
113 *Anne with Hermann and
Herbert Wilp.*

111 *Anne auf dem Dach des Hauses
am Merwedeplein, 1940.*
112 *Die Familie Frank auf dem
Merwedeplein, Mai 1940.*
113 *Anne mit Hermann und
Herbert Wilp.*

113

114

115

116

114 *Margot and Anne, 1940.*
115 *On the beach in Zandvoort,
August 1940.*
116 *Anne. 1940.*

114 *Margot und Anne.*
115 *In Zandvoort am Strand, 1940.*
116 *Anne, 1940.*

117 *Margot.*

1935

1935

1936

1937

1938

1939

1940

1941

1942

118 *Anne.*

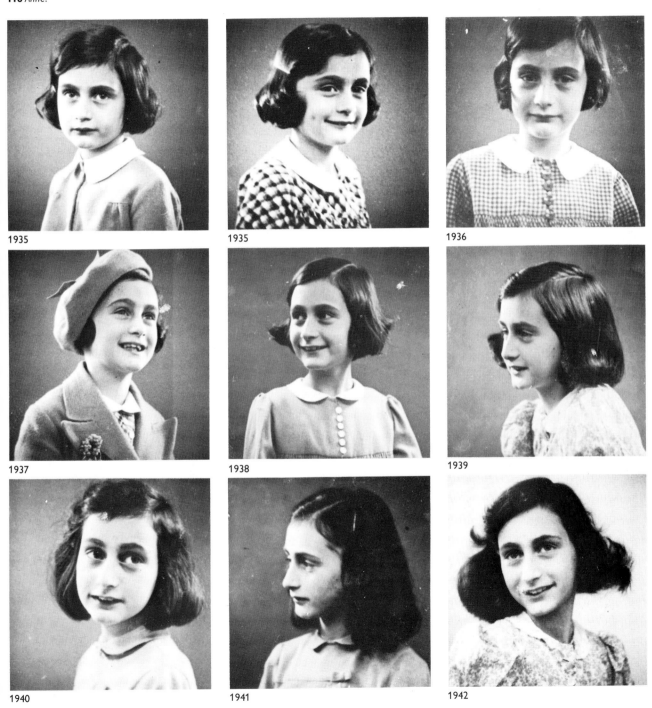

1935

1935

1936

1937

1938

1939

1940

1941

1942

72

The reactions from other countries to Hitler's seize of power differ markedly. Many do not believe he will stay in power for a long time and do not want to get involved. Others strongly oppose the developments in Germany. Still others are so enthusiastic about Hitler they organize National Socialist movements in their own country. In general, the danger of National Socialism and the persecution of the Jews is underestimated.

Hitlers Machtübernahme löst im Ausland ein sehr unterschiedliches Echo aus. Viele können sich überhaupt nicht vorstellen daß seine Regierung für längere Zeit Bestand hat. Andere dagegen protestieren gegen das NS-Regime. Einige bejubeln den Sieg des Nationalsozialismus und gründen im eigenen Land NS-Verbände. Im allgemeinen jedoch werden der Nationalsozialismus sowie das Ausmaß der Judenverfolgung stark unterschätzt.

120

121

119 As a protest against the mass arrests of socialists and communists, 18-year-old Sara Roth chains herself to a street lamp in Washington, D.C., 1933.
120 A plan to open Palestine to Jewish refugees. London, November 1938.
121 A branch of the SA is founded in California.

119 Washington, 1933: Sarah Roth kettet sich an eine Laterne, um gegen die massenhaften Verhaftungen deutscher Kommunisten und Sozialisten zu protestieren.
120 London, November 1938. Schaukästen mit Protestaufrufen gegen die Judenverfolgung sowie der Forderung nach einer Öffnung Palestinas für jüdische Flüchtlinge.
121 In vielen Ländern bilden sich NS-Sympathisantengruppen, die die NS-Ideologie übernehmen. Auch in den USA.

In 1931 Anton Mussert establishes the National Socialist Movement (NSB). In the '30s it becomes a growing political party, and in 1935 it captures nearly 8% of the vote. The following of the NSB consists of small businessmen, civil servants and farmers who have lost faith in the country's sectarian political parties.

After 1935 the popularity of the NSB diminishes, partly because of its acknowledged anti-Semitism. When Germany invades Holland the organization still has 27,000 members.

1931 gründet Anton Mussert die 'Nationaal Socialistische Beweging' (NSB). In der Folgezeit wächst die Bewegung zu einer Partei heran. Diese erringt 1935 knapp 8 Prozent aller Wählerstimmen. Die Anhänger rekrutieren sich vor allem aus der Beamtenschaft, dem Kleinbürgertum und Landwirten. Nach 1935 schwindet jedoch die Popularität der NSB. Ein Grund dafür ist der immer offener zu Tage tretende Antisemitismus. Trotzdem zählt die NSB 1940, als die Deutschen die Niederlande besetzen, noch 27 000 Mitglieder.

122 The NSB cadre pledge
allegiance to Mussert in Utrecht.
123 The NSB-youth organization:
The National Youth Storm.
124 NSB mass meeting.
125 The NSB is fiercely anti-
communist in the election
campaign: Mussert or Moscow.
126 'Fascism means action.'

122 Die Kader der NSB schwören
Mussert die Treue, Utrecht.
123 Die NSB-Jugendorganisation:
De Nationale Jeugdstorm.
124 Massenveranstaltung der NSB.
125 Ihre Wahlkampagnen richtet
die NSB vor allem gegen den
Bolschewismus: 'Entweder Mussert
oder Moskau'.
126 'Faschismus ist Tatkraft'.

124

125

123

126

29 MAY 1940: OCCUPATION OF HOLLAND

29 MAI 1940: DIE NIEDERLANDE BESETZT

The German invasion begins on May 10, 1940, and is a complete surprise. Holland expected to remain neutral as it had done during World War I.

The occupation is swift. In a few days all important areas are seized. The prime minister and his cabinet, as well as the Royal Family, fly to England. After fierce fighting near Arnhem and the bombing of Rotterdam, Holland is forced to surrender. As of May 15, 1940, the country is under German occupation.

Der Einmarsch der Deutschen kommt am 10. Mai 1940 für die meisten Niederländer völlig überraschend. Man hatte drauf gehofft, wie im ersten Weltkrieg, neutral bleiben zu können. Innerhalb weniger Tage ist das ganze Land unter deutscher Kontrolle. Nach heftigen Kämpfen bei Arnheim und der Zerstörung Rotterdams kapitulieren die nationalen Streitkräfte bedingungslos. Ab dem 15. Mai 1940 sind die Niederlande deutsches Besatzungsgebiet.

128

129

127 *German paratroopers land in Holland. May 10, 1940.*
128, 129 *The bombing of Rotterdam. More than 900 people are killed; more than 24,000 houses, destroyed.*
130 *Capitulation. Dutch soldiers turn in their weapons at Binnenhof, the seat of government in The Hague.*

127 *Deutsche Fallschirmspringer landen, 10. Mai 1940.*
128, 129 *Rotterdam wird zerstört: 900 Menschen sterben bei den Bomben-Angriffen und mehr als 24 000 Häuser werden zerstört.*
130 *Kapitulation. Auf dem Binnenhof in Den Haag (dem Parlament) geben niederländische Soldaten ihre Waffen ab.*

130

After the first shock and terror of the military actions, most Dutch are relieved that the Germans are behaving 'properly.' The majority of Dutch do not question the right of the Germans to impose their rules. Some measures taken by the Germans, like the blackouts, seem reasonable; others seem bearable, such as the introduction of the I.D. card. Since Germany seems invincible, it stands to reason one has to adapt to the inevitable. The large majority of civil servants, teachers and judges – as well as the Jews among them – fill out the 'Declaration of Aryanism.' The socialist trade union gets a NSB director, but most trade union leaders want to stay to salvage as much of their organization as possible. Thousands of members drop their union membership. A number of politicians establish a new political organization – the Dutch Union – which is anti-National Socialist but accepts the changed situation. In practice they do not oppose the German occupation. After a year, however, this union is also banned.

Nach der ersten Aufregung sind die meisten Niederländer erleichtert, daß sich die deutschen Besatzer so 'korrekt' verhalten. Einige der angeordneten Maßnahmen wie z.B. die Verdunklung stoßen auf Verständnis. Andere werden als gerade noch tragbar akzeptiert wie die Einführung eines Personalausweises. Die Verweigerung jeglicher Mitarbeit steht nicht ernsthaft zur Debatte. Man schickt sich ins Unvermeidbare, da Deutschland unbesiegbar scheint. Die überwiegende Mehrheit der Beamten – darunter auch die jüdischen – füllen den geforderten Ariernachweis aus. Der sozialistische Gewerkschaftsverband wird unter NSB-Führung gestellt. Die meisten Gewerkschaftsfunktionäre finden sich damit ab, in der Hoffnung, die Organisation so gut wie möglich retten zu können. Tausende von Mitgliedern verlassen allerdings die Gewerkschaft. Die christliche Gewerkschaft CNV löst sich selbst auf. Von drei Politikern wird eine neue politische Organisation ins Leben gerufen, die Niederländische Union. Binnen kurzer Zeit kann sie hunderttausende Mitglieder gewinnen. Diese Union ist zwar nicht nationalsozialistisch ausgerichtet, sie leistet aber auch keinen Widerstand gegen die Besatzer getreu der Überzeugung: 'Die Anerkennung der veränderten Verhältnisse ist notwendig'. Nach einer einjährigen Existenz neben der NSB wird die Union jedoch ebenso verboten wie zuvor die anderen politischen Parteien.

131

133

132

134

131 *Ration cards are needed to buy food.*
132 *Voting booths in Rotterdam are converted into dressing rooms.*
133 *Fences are erected along side the Amsterdam canals because the blackout makes walking dangerous at night.*
134 *Pigeons are captured and killed to prevent them from carrying messages. July 1940.*

131 *Einführung von Lebensmittelmarken.*
132 *Stimmkabinen werden in Rotterdam zu Badekabinen umgestaltet.*
133 *Durch die Verdunklung ist es nun nachts gefährlich, an den Grachten entlang zu laufen. Deshalb werden Geländer aufgestellt.*
134 *Brieftauben sind nicht mehr gestattet, weil sie Nachrichten übermitteln könnten. Juli 1940.*

135

135 *Nederlandse Unie (the Dutch Union) attracts hundreds of thousands of members quickly.*
136 *New measures are announced.*
137 *As of May 1941, every Dutch citizen is required to carry an identification card, a first for the Dutch. This registration takes place in Amsterdam.*
138 *Mayors are made aware of the Nazi ideology.*

135 *Die 'Niederländische Union'.*
136 *Neue Bekanntmachungen.*
137 *Seit Mai 1941 muss jeder Niederländer einen Personalausweis bei sich tragen. Vorher gab es keine. Amsterdam.*
138 *Nationalsozialistische Schulung für Bürgermeister.*

136

137

138

32 THE FIRST RAZZIA (ROUNDUP)   # 32 DIE ERSTE RAZZIA

That the Germans mean business becomes clear in February 1941. The W.A., the paramilitary arm of the NSB, repeatedly enters the Jewish neighborhood of Amsterdam, displaying aggressive and brutal behavior.
Markets on the Waterloo Square and at Amstelveld are raided. The inhabitants of the Jewish neighborhood organize groups to defend their property. Heavy fighting ensues.
When a W.A. man dies, the Germans retaliate. On February 22 the Jewish neighborhood is sealed off and 400 Jewish men and boys are grabbed off the streets and from houses and coffee shops, beaten and taken away. No one knows where to.

Im Februar 1941 wird klar, was die Besatzer beabsichtigen. Die WA, die Wehrabteilung der NSB, tritt immer häufiger und mit zunehmender Brutalität im Amsterdamer Judenviertel auf. Die Bewohner des Judenviertels bilden Schutzgruppen, um ihr Eigentum zu verteidigen. Es kommt zu heftigen Auseinandersetzungen. Als ein WA-Mann seinen dabei erlittenen Verletzungen erliegt, greifen die Deutschen hart durch. Am 22. Februar werden alle Ausgänge des Viertels gesperrt und beinahe 400 jüdische Jungen und Männer wahllos aus Häusern und Cafes gezerrt und abtransportiert. Noch ist nicht bekannt, wohin sie geführt werden.

139, 140 *The razzia on Jonas Daniël Meyer Square. February 22, 1941.*

139, 140 *Razzia auf dem Jonas Daniël Meijerplein.*

83

84

To protest against this *razzia*, a general strike is organized immediately, primarily by the Communist Party. In and around Amsterdam, thousands join in a two-day strike, making it the most influential act of resistance during the war. The Germans retaliate with force. German troops are sent in to restore order. Shots are fired. People are arrested. For fear of further reprisal, the strike is ended on February 27.

Aus Protest gegen die Razzia in Amsterdam rufen Widerstandsgruppen, insbesondere kommunistische, zu einem Generalstreik auf. Dieser Aufruf wird massenhaft befolgt: Am 25. und 26. Februar legen tausende von Arbeiter in und um Amsterdam die Arbeit nieder. Der Februarstreik wird zur zahlenmäßig größten Widerstandsaktion. Die Deutschen schlagen hart zurück: deutsche Truppenverbände werden nach Amsterdam geschickt. Auf die Menschenmassen wird scharf geschossen, viele werden verhaftet. Aus Angst vor Repressalien nimmt man am 27. Februar wieder die Arbeit auf.

Wij ontvingen heden het droeve bericht, dat onze geliefde Zoon, Broeder en Kleinzoon

ARNOLD HEILBUT,

in den leeftijd van 18 jaar, in Duitschland is overleden.

Amsterdam, 2 Juli 1941.
Z. Amstellaan 89.

H. M. HEILBUT.
F. HEILBUT—CARO
en familie.

Heden ontvingen wij bericht, dat in Duitschland op 25 Juni is overleden onze innig geliefde Zoon, Broeder en Zwager

AB. LOPES DE LEAÕ LAGUNA,

in den leeftijd van 24 jaar.
Namens de familie:

B. LOPES DE LEAÕ
LAGUNA.
Verzoeke geen bezoek.
Smaragdstraat 25 I Z.

Met diep leedwezen geven wij kennis, dat onze innig geliefde eenige Zoon

PAUL JACOBUS LEO,

in den ouderdom van 27 jaar, 25 Juni in Duitschland is overleden.

I. HEIMANS JR.
J. B. HEIMANS—
VAN GELDER.
Amsterdam, 1 Juli 1941.
Watteaustraat 5.

Liever geen rouwbeklag.

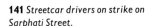

142

141 *Streetcar drivers on strike on Sarphati Street.*
142 *Several months after the razzia relatives of the arrested Jews receive death notices of their loved ones.*

141 *Streikende Strassenbahnfahrer in der Sarphatistraat.*
142 *Nur wenige Monate nach der Razzia kommen die ersten Todesnachrichten.*

141

The Dutch National Socialist organizations, of which the NSB is the largest, cooperate with the Germans. Even after the *razzia* in February they organize mass meetings to demonstrate their anti-Semitic and pro-German attitudes. There is also collaboration based on the self-interests of people who hope to profit from the German occupation in Holland. This ranges from selling cakes to the German Army to building military installations.

Die nationalsozialistischen Organisationen, deren größte die NSB ist, arbeiten eng mit den Deutschen zusammen. Sie organisieren auch noch nach den Razzien Massenversammlungen, auf denen sie ihre antisemitische Einstellung sowie ihre prodeutsche Gesinnung demonstrieren. Daneben gibt es auch Kollaboration aus Eigennutz: man erhofft sich materielle Vorteile. Das reicht vom Tortenverkauf an die Wehrmacht bis zum Bunkerbau.

143 *Mussert (center) and the German military leader Seyss Inquart inspect the German troops at the Binnenhof in The Hague.*
144 *NSB mass meeting on Museum Square, Amsterdam. June 27, 1941. Mussert: 'The German people can count on us as their most loyal guardian.'*
145 *1941: The windows of the New Israelitic Weekly are smashed.*

143 *Mussert (m.), Führer der NSB und Seyss-Inquart (l.) inspizieren die deutschen Truppen vor dem niederländischen Parlament in Den Haag.*
144 *27. Juni 1941. Massenkundgebung der NSB auf dem Amsterdamer Museumplein. Mussert: 'Das deutsche Volk kann auf uns zählen, wie auf seinen treuesten Hirten' ...Diese Kundgebung bildet nach dem Februarstreik den Auftakt einer neuen nationalsozialistischen Offensive zur Gewinnung von Anhängern.*
145 *Die Fensterscheiben der Wochenzeitung 'Nieuw Israëlitisch Weekblad' sind eingeworfen.*

144

143

145

146 The National Youth Storm is
the Dutch counterpart of the
German Hitler Youth. In spite of all
the money spent to create and
publish the propaganda, the
National Youth Storm does not
become a sizable organization
(12,000 members).

147 Dutch farmers are offered the
opportunity to settle in Poland and
parts of Russia. About 1,100
farmers decide to go. However,
most of them return disappointed,
and some are killed by Russian
partisans.

148 Dutch Nazi propaganda.

146 Der 'Nationale Jeugdstorm':
die niederländische Variante der
HJ. Trotz großen
Propagandaaufwandes erreicht er
nie die Stärke des NS-Vorbildes.
Der 'Jeugdstorm' kann nur 12000
Mitglieder gewinnen.

147 Das NS-Regime offeriert
niederländischen Bauern
Siedlungsland im Osten,
insbesondere in Polen und der
Ukraine. Partisanenangriffe
fordern unter den 1100 Bauern
zahlreiche Opfer. Enttäuscht
kehren viele wieder in die Heimat
zurück.

148 Niederländische
Nazipropaganda.

146

147

The Germans, using deep-rooted anti-communistic feelings, solicit volunteers for the war in Eastern Europe. No less than 30,000 Dutch men and boys sign up for the Waffen SS, and 17,000 are admitted beginning in April 1941. Another 15,000 volunteer for military auxiliary organizations and police groups.

Die Besatzer werben Freiwillige für den Krieg im Osten. Dabei wird vor allem auf den Antikommunismus gebaut. Immerhin 30000 Niederländer melden sich seit Juni 1941 bei der Waffen-SS. 17000 werden angemustert. Darüber hinaus bewerben sich noch 15000 Niederländer bei militärischen Hilfsorganisationen und Polizeieinheiten wie etwa dem 'Landstorm' oder der 'Landwacht'.

149

149 Volunteers departing for the Eastern Front in Russia. Inspection by General Seyffardt, The Hague. August 7, 1941.
150 Members of the NSB women's organization knit clothes for the volunteers at the Eastern Front.

149 Abfahrt Freiwilliger für die Ostfront, Musterung durch General Seyffardt, 7. August 1941.
150 Mitglieder der NSB-Frauenorganisation stricken für die Ostfrontfreiwilligen.

151 Volunteers departing for the Eastern Front in Russia. The Hague. July 1941.
152 Mussert visiting Dutch SS soldiers in Russia.
153 Dutch SS soldier at the front.

151 Abfahrt Freiwilliger an die Ostfront, Juli 1941.
152 Mussert (links) besucht SS-Freiwillige an der Front.
153 Niederländischer SS-Mann an der Front.

151

152

150

153

Germany lacks trained labor, especially after millions of Germans are drafted for the military service. During the occupation unemployed Dutchmen are forced to work in Germany. In May 1941 the number reaches 165,000.
In April 1942 a forced labor service is introduced for students and those who want to join the civil service. Many try to avoid the service. In the last years of the occupation the Germans seize men and boys at random from the streets and send them to Germany to work.

In Deutschland fehlen, seitdem die Wehrmacht enorm ausgeweitet worden ist, überall Facharbeiter. Während der Besatzung werden arbeitslose Niederländer zum Arbeitseinsatz in Deutschland gezwungen. Im Mai 1941 sind das schon 165 000 Personen. Im April 1942 führen die Deutschen die 'Arbeitsdienstpflicht' für Studenten und Beamtenanwärter ein. Viele versuchen sich davor zu drücken. Gegen Ende des Krieges spitzt sich die Lage sogar so zu, dass die Deutschen wahllos Jungen und Männer von der Strasse aufgreifen und in Deutschland einsetzen.

154

154 'Workers in the metal industry! Wouldn't you like to work here? That can be arranged!'
155 Recruitment agency which arranges for the Dutch to work in Germany.

154 'Metallarbeiter! Möchten Sie hier nicht gerne arbeiten? Kein Problem...'
155 Vermittlungsstelle für Arbeit in Deutschland. – 'im Ausland'.

156 *Propaganda photos imitating the German example of the Labor Service.*
157 *Dutch workers in Germany. Photos are intended for publication in Holland.*

156 *Für den Arbeitsdienst Propagandafotos nach deutschem Vorbild.*
157 *Niederländische Arbeiter in Deutschland. Diese Fotos sind für die Heimat bestimmt.*

156

155

157

94

In January 1941 the Germans force prominent Jews to form a Jewish council, which has to represent all Jews. They agree to do so in hopes of avoiding worse. The Germans use the Jewish Council as a means to execute their orders. Step by step the rights of Jews are limited, and the Jewish community is gradually isolated.

Am 12. Februar 1941 fordern die Besatzungsbehörden prominente Juden auf, einen 'Jüdischen Rat' zu bilden. Er soll fortan alle Juden vertreten. Man stimmt zu in der Meinung, damit 'Schlimmeres verhüten' zu können. Aber die Besatzer nutzen den Rat als Instrument für die Durchsetzung ihrer Maßnahmen. Schritt für Schritt werden die Rechte der Juden eingeschränkt, und die jüdische Gemeinschaft gerät in eine immer stärkere gesellschaftliche Isolation.

158 A grocery store: 'Jews not allowed.'
159 By February 1943 most of the shops in the Jewish ghetto are already closed.

158 Lebensmittelladen: 'Für Juden verboten'.
159 Februar 1943. Im jüdischen Viertel sind die meisten Läden geschlossen.

158

159

160 Identification cards of Jews are stamped with a 'J.' Summer 1941.
161 A swimming pool: 'Jews not allowed.'

160 Sommer 1941: In die Personalausweise der Juden wird ein grosses 'J' gestempelt. Zuvor waren schon die Einwohnermeldekarten gekennzeichnet worden.
161 Schwimmbad: 'für Juden verboten'.

160

161

163

164

162

162 *The opposite of the 'Jews not allowed' sign: 'Jews only.' Waterloo Square Market, Amsterdam.*
163 *Jewish artists fired from their jobs advertise their availability to give concerts or performances. These can be given in Jewish households only.*
164 *A wedding.*
165 *In a synagogue.*

162 *Entweder: 'Verboten für Juden' oder wie hier: 'Nur für Juden'.*
163 *Jüdische Künstler, die arbeitslos geworden sind, bieten sich für Hauskonzerte an. Jedoch nur bei Juden.*
164 *Hochzeit.*
165 *In der Synagoge.*

165

98

Although most Dutchmen are anti-German or become that way once they are confronted with shortages and terror, this does not imply they automatically choose to join the Resistance. Many factors immobilize them: fear, a fundamental rejection of civil disobedience, and religious principles based on the need to obey any government in power. But mostly the (false) choices between fascism and communism immobilize the Dutch. For those who do resist, political and religious differences hamper the coordination of the Resistance, especially in the first year of the occupation. There is no preparation for the occupation, let alone a tradition of resistance among the Dutch. The first acts of resistance are mostly symbolic. In 1942 and 1943 a more efficient resistance movement develops.

Obwohl die überwiegende Mehrheit der Niederländer antideutsch eingestellt ist, nicht zuletzt aufgrund der Mangelwirtschaft und des Terrors, führt dies keineswegs automatisch zu einer Entscheidung, sich dem Widerstand anzuschließen. Verschiedene Faktoren spielen dabei eine Rolle: Angst, grundsätzliche Ablehnung bürgerlichen Ungehorsams, religiöse Überzeugungen, daß man sich der weltlichen Macht zu fügen habe und vor allem die von den Nazis raffiniert propagierte Scheinalternative: Kommunismus oder Faschismus. Unter denen, die in den Widerstand gehen, erschweren anfangs politische und religiöse Meinungsverschiedenheiten die Zusammenarbeit. Zudem ist man auf die Besatzung schlecht vorbereitet. Erst im Laufe der Jahre 1942 und 1943 kommt es zur planmäßigen Organisierung des Widerstands.

166

167

166, 167, 168 An important activity of the Dutch resistance is the underground press. People listen to the Allied Radio stations, and the news is spread by underground stenciled or printed bulletins. About 30,000 people are involved in this activity.

166, 167, 168 Zu den wichtigsten Stützen des Widerstands gehören illegale Zeitungen. In ihnen erscheinen Berichte ausländischer Radiosender. An der Erstellung sowie dem Verteilen der Zeitungen sind rund 30000 Niederlander beteiligt.

168

41, 42 THE BEGINNING OF THE DEPORTATIONS: GOING INTO HIDING, BETRAYAL AND RESISTANCE

41, 42 DER BEGINN DER DEPORTATIONEN: UNTERTAUCHEN, VERRAT UND WIDERSTAND

Starting in January 1942 unemployed Jewish men are called upon to report for work in eastern Holland. Next, not only men, but entire families are summoned to go to Westerbork, a camp that serves as a collection point. From there they are transported to what were called labor camps.

The Jewish Council is pressured to deliver the required numbers for transportation to Westerbork. When the quotas are not met, Jews are arrested at random. Thousands of Jews decide not to go and try to hide.

Seit Januar 1942 werden arbeitslose jüdische Jungen und Männer zur 'Arbeitsbeschaffung' in Drenthe eingezogen. Bald darauf werden ganze Familien ins Lager Westerbork abtransportiert. Von dort werden viele per Zug in 'Arbeitslager' im Osten verschickt.

Der Jüdische Rat wird aufgefordert, die festgelegten Transportquoten für Westerbork einzuhalten. Unterschreitungen führen zu willkürlichen Razzien. Tausende Juden folgen den Aufforderungen, sich zu melden, nicht und versuchen unterzutauchen.

169 Where to hide? Only a few Jews can find a hiding place. Here, Jewish children hide at the farm of the Boogaard family.
170 During the entire month of August 1942 the razzias continue.

169 Untertauchen, aber wo? Nur wenige finden ein Versteck. Hier jüdische Kinder, die auf dem Land bei der Familie Boogaard untergetaucht sind.
170 Im gesamten Monat August 1942 kommt es zu Razzien.

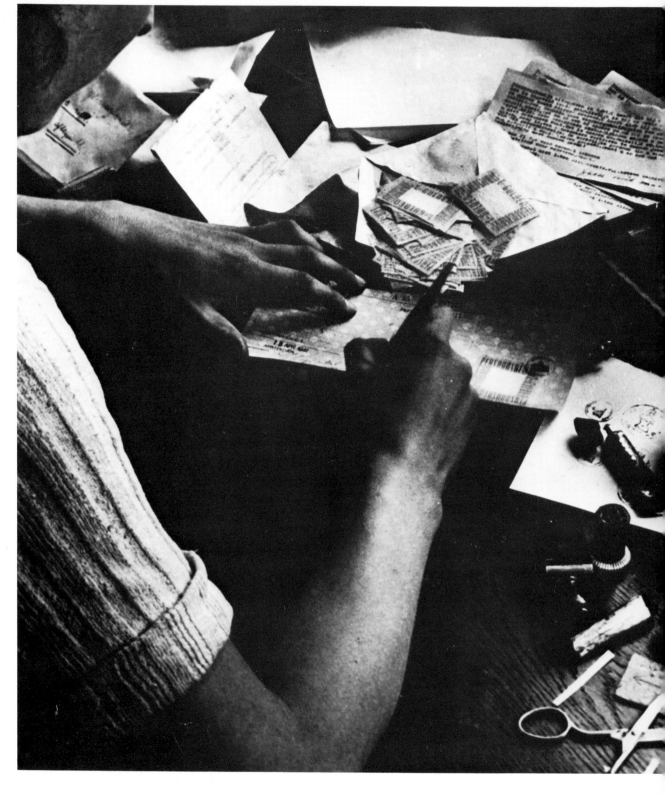

171 *Falsification of identity papers, 1942.*
172 *The files from the registration office of the town of Jisp are hidden.*
173 *The registration office, where vital statistics of the population are kept, is demolished by a resistance group. Amsterdam.*

171 *Personalausweise werden gefälscht.*

172 *Das Einwohnermeldeamtsbuch von Jisp verschwindet.*
173 *Das Einwohnermeldeamt von Amsterdam wird von einer Widerstandsgruppe in die Luft gejagt.*

171

172

173

THE FRANK FAMILY *GOING INTO HIDING*

DIE FAMILIE FRANK *UNTERTAUCHEN*

During 1941 the number of anti-Jewish measures increases, and the Franks start preparing to go into hiding. Thanks to the cooperation of his staff (Mr. Kraler, Mr. Koophuis, Miep Gies and Elli Vossen), Otto Frank is able to secretly prepare a hiding place for his family and the van Daans (Mr. van Daan works with Otto Frank's company.)
On July 5, 1942, Margot Frank receives the notorious call to report to a 'labor camp.' The next day the Frank family moves into the 'Secret Annex.' One week later Mr. and Mrs. van Daan and their son Peter join them, followed by Mr. Dussel.

Im Laufe des Jahres 1941 nehmen die antijüdischen Maßnahmen der Besatzer zu, und die Familie Frank beginnt mit den Vorbereitungen für das Untertauchen. Dank der Mitarbeit seiner Angestellten, Kraler, Koophuis, Miep Gies und Elli Vossen, schafft Otto Frank es, im Geheimen ein Versteck für seine Familie und die Familie van Daan vorzubereiten (Herr van Daan ist an Otto Franks Geschäft beteiligt).
Am 5. Juli 1942 erhält Margot die berüchtigte Einberufung zum 'Arbeitseinsatz'. Schon am nächsten Tag taucht die Familie Frank unter. Eine Woche später folgen Herr und Frau van Daan mit ihrem Sohn Peter. Ein paar Monate später kommt noch Herr Dussel hinzu. Die Geschehnisse der folgenden Jahre hat Anne in ihrem Tagebuch festgehalten. Sie hatte es zum 13. Geburtstag geschenkt bekommen.

175

174 The Annex, the hiding place.
175 The people in hiding: Otto, Edith, Anne and Margot Frank. Mr. and Mrs. van Daan, Peter van Daan and Mr. Dussel.
176 The helpers of the people in hiding, from left to right: Mr. Koophuis, Miep Gies, Elli Vossen and Mr. Kraler.

174 Das Hinterhaus.
175 Die Untergetauchten: Otto, Edith, Anne und Margot Frank. Untere Reihe: Herr und Frau van Daan, Sohn Peter und Herr Dussel.
176 Die Helfer der Untertauchten. V.l.n.r.: Koophuis, Miep Gies, Elli Vossen und Kraler.

176

177 *Anne Frank's room.* Our little room looked very bare at first with nothing on the walls; but thanks to Daddy who had brought my film star collection and picture postcards on beforehand, and with the aid of paste pot and brush, I have transformed the walls into one gigantic picture. This makes it look much more cheerful. *(Anne writing in her diary on July 11, 1942.)*

178 The entrance to our hiding place has now been properly concealed. Mr. Kraler thought it would be better to put a cupboard in front of our door (because a lot of houses are being searched for hidden bicycles), but of course it had to be a movable cupboard that can open like a door. Mr. Vossen made the whole thing. *(Anne writing in her diary on August 21, 1944.) The picture shows Mr. Koophuis next to the bookcase.*

179 *The attic of the Annex, where Anne wrote her diary most of the time.*

177 *Anne Franks Zimmer.* 'Unser Zimmer war bisher ganz kahl. Glücklicherweise hat Vater meine ganze 'Filmstar- und Ansichtskartensammlung' mitgenommen, und ich habe mit Leim und Pinsel schöne Bilderwände gemacht. Nun sieht es sehr lustig bei uns aus.' *Anne in ihrem Tagebuch am 11. Juli 1942.*

178 'Herr Kraler hatte die gute Idee, die Eingangstür zu unserem Hinterhaus zu verbauen, weil soviele Haussuchungen nach Fahrrädern gehalten werden. Den Plan ausgeführt hat Herr Vossen: Er hat ein drehbares Regal gemacht, das sich nach einer Seite als Tür öffnet.' *Anne in ihrem Tagebuch am 21. August 1942. Auf dem Foto Herr Koophuis vor dem Bücherregal.*

179 *Der Dachboden des Hinterhauses. Hier schreibt Anne meistens in ihr Tagebuch.*

177

178

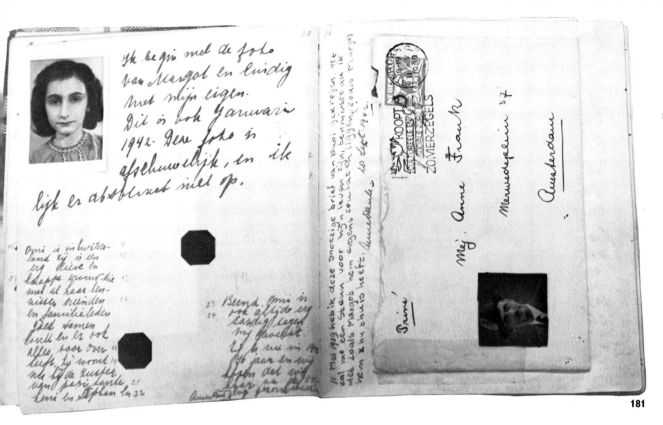

181

182

180 *View of the Prinsengracht, Westerkerk and the Annex.* Daddy, Mummy, and Margot can't get used to the sound of the Westertoren clock yet, which tells us the time every quarter of an hour. I can. I loved it from the start, and especially in the night it's like a faithful friend. *(Anne writing in her diary on July 11, 1942.)*

181 *Page from Anne's first diary.*

182 Believe me, if you have been shut up for a year and a half, it can get too much for you some days. In spite of all justice and thankfulness, you can't crush your feelings. Cycling, dancing, whistling, looking out into the world, feeling young, to know that I'm free – that's what I long for; still, I mustn't show it, because I sometimes think if all eight of us began to pity ourselves, or went about with discontented faces, where would it lead us? *(Anne writing in her diary, on December 24, 1943.)*

180 *Luftaufnahme von der Prinsengracht, der Westerkerk und dem Hinterhaus.*
'Vater, Mutter und Margot können sich immer noch nicht an das Läuten der Westerturm-Glocke gewöhnen, die jede Viertelstunde schlägt. Ich schon, ich finde es sogar sehr schön und besonders nachts hat es etwas Beruhigendes.' *Anne in ihrem Tagebuch am 11. Juli 1942.*

181 *Seite aus Annes erstem Tagebuch.*

182 'Glaube mir, wenn man eineinhalb Jahre so eingeschlossen sitzt, wird es manchmal zuviel. Mag es auch unrecht und undankbar sein, aber Gefühle lassen sich nicht verleugnen. Tanzen möchte ich, pfeifen, radeln, die Welt sehen, meine Jugend geniessen, frei sein. Das sage ich hier, aber zeigen darf ich es nicht. Denn wenn wir alle nun alle acht klagten und mit unglücklichen Gesichtern herumliefen, wohin sollte das führen?' *Anne in ihrem Tagebuch am 24. Dezember 1943.*

In the spring of 1943 the German military loses ground. Allied advances in North Africa, the Soviet counterattack and the fall of Mussolini stimulate the Resistance. But simultaneously repression for the remaining Dutchmen is increased.
In September 1944 among the non-Jewish population 250,000 are hiding; 12,500 are prisoners of war; 7,000, political prisoners; and 300,000, forced laborers. Aside from those groups, about 900,000 people are forced to leave their homes and move. The total population in Holland then is about nine million. Starting in the summer of 1944, many resistance fighters are summarily shot. Hundreds of others are executed in retaliation for acts of resistance.

Im Frühjahr 1943 kommt der Vormarsch der deutschen Wehrmacht zum stehen. Die Eroberung von Teilen Nordafrikas durch die alliierten Truppen, die erfolgreiche sowjetische Gegenoffensive sowie der Sturz Mussolinis ermutigen den Widerstand. Die Aktionen nehmen zu. Zugleich wird die Repression gegen die noch übriggebliebene Bevölkerung verschärft. Im September 1944 sind von den nicht-jüdischen Niederländern 250 000 untergetaucht, 12 500 sind Kriegsgefangene, 7 000 politische Häftlinge und 300 000 Zwangsarbeiter. Etwa 900 000 Menschen werden gezwungen, ihre Häuser zu verlassen und umzuziehen. Die Gesamtbevölkerung der Niederlande ist dann ungefähr 9 Millionen.

184

185

183 The liquidation of a traitor. Resistance groups have emotional discussions whether one has the right to execute traitors.
184 In 1943 and 1944 thousands of men are sent to Germany to work.
185 Many men and young adults go into hiding, mostly at farms to escape being forced to work in Germany.

183 Liquidierung eines Verräters. Innerhalb der Widerstandsbewegung sind die Meinungsunterschiede gross, ob man einen Verräter überhaupt liquidieren darf.
184 Tausende werden 1943 und 1944 zum Arbeitseinsatz nach Deutschland verschleppt.
185 Viele versuchen sich dem Arbeitseinsatz in Deutschland durch die Flucht aufs Land zu entziehen.

186 *The marriage party of Ger de Beer and Ina Verkuyl in 1943. Both families are active in the resistance and many of the guests, as well. Father Verkuyl, his son and Ger de Beer are executed in 1944.*
187 *Executed resistance fighters.*
188 *In September 1944, the Dutch Railway workers go on strike. German trains are attacked by sabotage groups.*

186 *Hochzeit zwischen Geer de Beer und Ina Verkuijl, 1943. Beide Familien sind im Widerstand tätig, viele Gäste ebenso. Der Vater von Ina Verkuijl, ihr Bruder und ihr Bräutigam werden 1944 erschossen.*
187 *Hingerichtete Widerstandskämpfer.*
188 *September 1944: Das Personal der niederländischen Eisenbahn streikt. Es kommt zu Sabotage gegen Züge der Reichsbahn.*

186

187

45 DEPORTATION OF THE JEWS

45 DEPORTATIONEN NACH WESTERBORK

Most *razzias* and transportation activity to the camps occur at night.
In Amsterdam most Jews are first brought to the Jewish Theater and then on to Westerbork.
The majority stay there several weeks, some more than a year. In 1943 one transport follows another until the camp is full and life becomes unbearable. Westerbork, however, is not a final destination. Rather, it is a collection point to transport the Jews to the extermination camps.

Die meisten Razzien und Abtransporte finden abends statt. In Amsterdam werden die Juden erst zum jüdischen Theater gebracht und von dort aus nach Westerbork. Dort bleiben die Deportierten zumeist einige Wochen, manche aber auch länger als ein Jahr. Im Laufe des Jahres 1943 nimmt die Zahl der Transporte enorm zu, und das Lager ist ständig überfüllt. Aber Westerbork ist ein Durchgangslager auf dem Weg nach Osten.

189

190

189 *Waiting for the departure to Westerbork, Amsterdam. May 26 1943. The photographs were taken for an SS magazine.*
190 *Departure from Amsterdam's Muiderpoort Station to Westerbork.*
191 *Westerbork, the Dutch transit camp.)*

189 *Amsterdam, Sammlung zum Transport nach Westerbork. Diese Fotos vom 26. Mai 1943 sind im Auftrag einer SS Zeitschrift gemacht worden.*
190 *Transport nach Westerbork (Muiderpoort Bahnhof).*
191 *Durchgangslager Westerbork.*

191

46 D-DAY AND THE LIBERATION OF SOUTHERN HOLLAND

46 D-DAY, DOLLER DIENSTAG UND DIE BEFREIUNG DER SUDNIEDERLANDE

In 1944 the Allied Forces gain momentum in Europe. The Germans retreat from Eastern Europe. The liberation of Western Europe begins with D-Day. In one day, June 6, 1944, 156,000 Allied soldiers land in northern France.
Following the successful invasion, rumors about the liberation begin. In Holland on September 5, 1944, known as 'Mad Tuesday,' most people believe the liberation is near. Southern Holland is, in reality, liberated.

Im Laufe des Jahres 1944 werden die Deutschen an allen Fronten zurückgeschlagen. In Osteuropa rücken die sowjetischen Truppen rasch vor, und in Westeuropa landen am 6. Juni 1944 in der Normandie 156 000 alliierte Soldaten. In den Niederlanden kommen zahlreiche Gerüchte über eine unmittelbar bevorstehende Befreiung auf. Nicht zuletzt aufgrund allzu optimistischer englischer Rundfunkberichte glauben viele Menschen, daß der Krieg so gut wie vorbei ist. Es kommt am 5. September 1944 zum 'Dollen Dienstag': Spott und Prügel für Kollaborateure und Besatzer. Wochen darauf wird der Süden des Landes tatsächlich befreit.

192

193

194

192 D-Day (Decision Day): American and English troops land in Normandy, France. June 6, 1944.
193 September 5, 1944, known as 'Wild Tuesday.' NSB members hurry to leave Holland. The Hague Railway station.
194 'Wild Tuesday': The village of Rijswijk waits in vain for the Allied troops to come.
195 Allied soldiers hand out chewing gum.

192 D-Day (Decision Day): Landung amerikanischer und englischer Truppenverbände an der Nordfranzösischen Küste, 6. Juni 1944.
193 'Doller Dienstag', 5. September 1944. Flüchtende NSB-Männer im Bahnhof Den Haag.
194 Die Bevölkerung Rijswijks warten am 'dollen Dienstag' vergeblich auf die alliierten Befreier.
195 Alliierte Soldaten verteilen im Süden des Landes Kaugummi.

195

118

The Dutch Railway halts service in September 1944 because of a railway strike ordered by the Dutch government in exile in London. As a result, the Germans retaliate by forbidding food to be brought to the cities. An enormous shortage results, worsened by food confiscated by the Germans. When coal and other fuel are not delivered to the cities, the situation becomes critical. Everything that can burn is used for heat. Everything edible is eaten, even tulip bulbs. Thousands of children are sent to the countryside to be fed. About 22,000 people die of hunger. Tens of thousands are seriously ill. Meanwhile, the Germans take anything of value to Germany: bicycles, machines, factory equipment, streetcars and cattle, for example.

September 1944: Eisenbahnerstreik, zu dem die niederländische Exilregierung in London aufgerufen hatte. Zur Strafe verbieten die Deutschen alle Lebensmitteltransporte in die großen Städte. Die Nahrungsmittelnot wird zusätzlich durch Beschlagnahmungen der Besatzer verschärft. Als schließlich auch keine Brennstoffe mehr geliefert werden, wird die Lage besonders kritisch. Alles Brennbare wird verheizt, alles Eßbare verschlungen: sogar Tulpenzwiebeln kommen auf den Teller. Tausende von Kindern werden auf dem Land untergebracht. In diesem Winter sterben 22000 Menschen vor Hunger. Die Besatzer schleppen alles ab, was ihnen wertvoll erscheint: Maschinen, Straßenbahnwagen, Vieh, Fahrräder usw.

197

198

196 *Children remove an old door for firewood.*
197 *People even burn wood from their own houses.*
198 *Hungry children.*
199 *In the countryside thousands of people try to exchange goods for food.*

196 *Kinder sammeln Holz.*
197 *Sogar das Holz in der eigenen Wohnung muss zum Heizen herhalten.*
198 *Hungernde Kinder.*
199 *Tausende ziehen aufs Land und versuchen Wertgegenstände gegen Nahrung zu tauschen.*

199

When Germany marches through Eastern Europe, the army is followed by SS special units (*Einsatz Gruppen*) that start the mass execution of Jews. More than one million Jews are shot. In 1941 the decision is made 'to make Europe clean of Jews.' During the Wannsee Conference in January 1942 plans are made to annihilate the 11 million European Jews. The plans become known as the *Endlösung,* the 'final solution of the Jewish question.' Destruction and labor camps are built. A large number of the deported Jews – mostly the elderly, mothers and children – are gassed immediately upon arrival. The others must work a couple of months until they die of exhaustion. In this way nearly six million Jews are killed. In addition to the Jews, countless others die in the concentration camps: political opponents, homosexuals, Jehovah's Witnesses, 'anti-social elements,' Russian prisoners of war and at least 220,000 gypsies.

Den deutschen Truppenverbänden in Ost-Europa folgen sogenannte 'Einsatzgruppen': SS, die mit der Ausrottung der Juden beginnt. Bei Massenexekutionen erschiesst die SS mehr als eine Million Juden. 1941: Auf der 'Wannsee-Konferenz' planen führende Nazis die 'Endlösung der Judenfrage' – die systematische Ausrottung 11 Millionen europäischer Juden. Hierfür werden spezielle Vernichtungslager errichtet. Während Mütter mit Kindern sowie alte Menschen aussortiert und in Gaskammern getrieben werden, werden alle 'Arbeitsfähigen' in Baracken zusammengepfercht und von morgens bis abends zu Schwerstarbeit eingesetzt. Die meisten sterben an Unterernährung, Erschöpfung, fallen Krankheiten zum Opfer. Auf diese Weise werden etwa 6 Millionen Juden in den Konzentrationslagern umgebracht. Darüber hinaus sterben noch zahllose andere Opfer der Nazis in den Lagern: politische Gegner, Homosexuelle, Zeugen Jehovas, sogenannte 'Assoziale', russische Kriegsgefangene und viele andere. In den Lagern werden auch mindestens 220 000 Zigeuner ermordet.

201

200 *Dutch Jews departing from Westerbork for Auschwitz.*
201 *Jews in Eastern Europe are rounded up by special command groups (Einsatzgruppen) and murdered.*

200 *Niederländische Juden auf dem Weg von Westerbork nach Auschwitz.*
201 *Osteuropäische Juden werden durch die 'Einsatzgruppen' zusammengetrieben und ermordet.*

202

202 *Upon arrival in Auschwitz Jews are divided into two groups: those who can still work and those who are to be exterminated immediately.*

203 *The IG Farben Co. operates on enormous manufacturing site near Auschwitz. The death toll among the forced labourers at this site is extremely high.*

204 *A gas chamber in Majdanek destruction camp.*

205 *The possessions of those who have been exterminated are sorted, and anything of valuable is salvaged i.e. locks of hair and gold-filled teeth.*

203

204

205

202 *Bei der Ankunft in Auschwitz wird sofort selektiert, wer noch arbeiten kann, oder gleich vergast wird.*

203 *Die Firma I.G.-Farben hat eine Fabrik in der Nähe des Lager, in der Gefangene arbeiten. Die Sterbequoten sind erschreckend hoch.*

204 *Die Gaskammer im Vernichtungslager Majdanek.*

205 *Bei der Ankunft werden die Häftlinge geschoren, ihre gesamte Habe wird konfisziert und sortiert. Den Toten werden die Goldzähne rausgerissen.*

On August 4, 1944, the German police make a raid on the 'Secret Annex.' All the occupants are arrested and sent to concentration camps.

Am 4. August 1944 fällt die 'Grüne Polizei' ins Hinterhaus ein, arrestiert alle Versteckten und bringt sie in deutsche Konzentrationslager.

206 The train from Westerbork to Auschwitz.
207 A list of deportees on the last train from Westerbork to Auschwitz contains the names of the Frank family.
Mrs. Edith Frank-Holländer is killed by the hardships of Auschwitz. Mr. van Daan dies in the gaschamber. Peter van Daan is taken by the SS when the concentration camp was abandoned because of the approach of the Russians. He dies in Mauthausen. Mr. Dussel dies in the Neuengamme concentrationcamp. At the end of October Margot and Anne are transported back in Germany, to Bergen-Belsen. Both of them contract typhus. They die in March 1945. Mrs. van Daan also dies in Bergen-Belsen. Otto Frank is liberated by the Russian troops at Auschwitz.

206 Der Zug Westerbork-Auschwitz.
207 Die Transportliste des letzten Zuges, der nach Auschwitz fuhr. Auf der Liste stehen die Namen der Familie Frank.
Frau Edith Frank-Holländer stirbt im Konzentrationslager Auschwitz an den Entbehrungen. Herr van Daan wird vergast. Peter wird von der SS mitgeführt, als das Lager wegen der aufrückenden russischen Truppen geräumt wird. Er stirbt später in Mauthausen. Herr Dussel stirbt im Lager Neuengamme. Anne und Margot werden im Oktober des Jahres 1944 ins Lager Bergen-Belsen gebracht. Dort verbringen sie den Winter. Doch sie infizieren sich beide mit Typhus und sterben kurz hintereinander im März 1945. Im gleichen Lager stirbt auch Frau van Daan. Als einziger Überlebender der Untergetauchten erlebt Otto Frank die Befreiung des Lagers Auschwitz durch die Russen.

206

JUDENTRANSPORT AUS DEN NIEDERLANDEN - LAGER WESTERBORK

Haeftlinge

301. ✓Engers	Isidor —	✓30.4. 93 –	Kaufmann
302✓ Engers	Leonard	15.6. 20 –	Lamdarbeiter
303✓ Franco	Manfred –	✓1.5. 05 –	Verleger
304. Frank	Arthur	22.8. 81	Kaufmann
305. Frank ✗	Isaac	✓29.11.87	Installateur
306. Frank	Margot	16.2. 26	ohne
307. Frank ✓	Otto	✓12.5. 89	Kaufmann
308.✓ Frank-Hollaender	Edith	16.1. 00	ohne
309. Frank	Anneliese	12.6. 29	ohne
310. v.Franck	Sara –	27.4. 02 –	Typistin
311. Franken	Rozanna	16.5. 96 –	Landarbeiter
312.✓ Franken-Weyand	Johanna	24.12.96✓	Landbauer
313. Franken	Hermann –	✓12.5.34	ohne
314. Franken	Louis	10.8. 17 –	Gaertner
315. Franken ℛ	Rosalina	29.3. 27	Landbau
316. Frankfort	Alex	14.11.19 –	Dr.i.d.Oekonomie
317. Frankfort-Elsas	Regina	11.12.19	Apoth-.Ass.
318. Frankfoort ✗	Elias	✓22.10.98 –	Schneider
319.✓Frankfort ℛ	Max	20.6. 21	Schneider
320.✓Frankfort-Weijl ℛ	Hetty	29.3. 24	Naeherin
321.✓Frankfort-Werkendam ℛ	Rosette	24.6.98	Schriftstellerin
322.✓ Frijda	Hermann	22.6. 87 –	Hochschullehrer
323. Frenk	Henriette	28.4. 21	Typistin
324. Frenk ℛ	Rosa	15.3.24	Haushalthilfe
325. Friezer	Isaac	10.3. 20 –	Korrespondent
326.✓ Fruitman-Vlessche-			
drager ℛ	Fanny	24.1. 03	ohne
327. Gans ✗	Elie	✓24.10.03 –	Betriebleiter
328. Gans-Koopman ℛ	Gesina	20.12.05	Maschinestrickerin
329. Gans	Kalman –	6.3. 79	Diamantarbeiter
330. Gans ℛ	Klara	12.5. 13	Naeherin
331. Gans ·	Paul –	27.9. 08 –	Landbauer
332. v.Gelder	Abraham –	9.11.78	Metzger
333. v.Gelder-de Jong	Reintje	22.10.81	ohne
334. v.Gelder	Alexander	27.6. 03 –	Kaufmann

50 THE STARVING ENDS AS HOLLAND IS LIBERATED

50 DIE BEFREIUNG DER NIEDERLANDE

In April 1945 the English are allowed to drop food over starving Holland, allowing many thousands to survive. The announcement is made over British radio.
A few weeks later the war is over. The remainder of Holland is liberated by the Allied Forces. Festivities are organized throughout the country. At the same time the Nazis and their collaborators are arrested.

Die englische Luftwaffe wirft gegen Ende April 1945 Nahrungspakete über Holland ab. Die Aktionen werden über die englischen Sender angekündigt und sind sehr willkommen: tausende überleben so den Krieg, der schon wenige Wochen später beendet ist. Am 5. Mai 1945 werden die restlichen Niederlande befreit. Im ganzen Land feiert man das Ende der deutschen Besatzung. Es kommt zu ersten Verhaftungen von NSB-Anhängern und Kollaborateuren.

208 *English bombers loaded with parcels of food above Rotterdam. April 30, 1945.*
209 *Liberation festivities in Amsterdam's Red Light District.*

208 *Englische Bomberwerfer mit Nahrungspaketen über Rotterdam, 30.4.1945.*
209 *Die ganze Stadt Amsterdam feiert die Befreiung: im Vergnügungsviertel.*

209

128

On May 8, 1945, the German Army surrenders unconditionally. During the last months of the war German cities are so heavily bombed that little remains. Hitler and Goebbels commit suicide. Many Nazis are arrested.
The Soviet, American and other Allied troops work closely to defeat Nazi Germany.
Although the liberation comes too late for millions, many in prisons and concentration camps can be saved.
Germany is brought under joint Allied authority.

Am 8. Mai 1945 kapituliert das deutsche Heer bedingungslos. Nach schweren Bombardements der vorangegangen Monate liegen große Teile der deutschen Städte in Schutt und Asche. Hitler und Goebbels begehen in Berlin Selbstmord. Viele Nazis werden verhaftet. Bei der Eroberung Deutschlands arbeiten die USA, England, Frankreich und die Sowjetunion eng zusammen.
Obwohl die Hilfe für Millionen zu spät kommt, können die Eroberer viele aus Gefängnissen und Konzentrationslagern befreien. Bis auf weiteres wird Deutschland alliiertes Besatzungsgebiet.

210

210 *In the German countryside Americans say hello to the Russians.*
211 *Soviet and U.S. troops meet at the Elbe River in Germany.*
212 *Frankfurt.*
213 *Jewish survivors, liberated from Theresiënstadt, return to Frankfurt.*
214 *Some very young boys, members of the Hitler Youth, are among the arrested soldiers.*

210 *Irgendwo in Deutschland: Amerikaner grüssen Russen.*
211 *Sowjetische und amerikanische Truppen treffen sich an der Elbe.*
212 *Das zerstörte Frankfurt.*
213 *Jüdische Überlebende aus Theresienstadt kehren nach Frankfurt zurück.*
214 *'Das letzte Aufgebot des Führers': die Hitlerjugend.*

212

213

211

214

52 LIBERATION OF THE CONCENTRATION CAMPS

52 BEFREIUNG DER KONZENTRATIONSLAGER UND HEIMKEHR DER HÄFTLINGE

The Allied advance into Germany influences the situation at the concentration camps. In January 1945 the Nazis clear the camps by forcing prisoners to walk hundreds of miles through snow and rain. Thousands die.

What the Allied Forces find when they finally arrive at the concentration camps is indescribable. For the survivors, a difficult journey home begins. For many of them the homecoming is a bitter disappointment. Most have lost friends and family. Houses are occupied. Property is stolen. Many survivors encounter disbelief and ignorance about their experiences in the camps.

Als sich die alliierten Truppen den Lagern nähern, werden diese geräumt. Oftmals werden die Häftlinge gezwungen, mit den abrückenden Wachmannschaften mitzuziehen. Tausende sterben auf diesen Todesmärschen durch Schnee und Regen. Die Alliierten finden, als sie die Lager befreien, grauenhafte Verhältnisse vor. Für die Überlebenden beginnt nun eine schwierige Reise nach Hause. Die Heimkehr endet oftmals mit einer bitteren Enttäuschung: Familie und Freunde sind umgekommen. Der Besitz geraubt. Die Zurückgebliebenen können zudem das Ausmaß der Leiden, die die Häftlinge erfahren haben, nicht ermessen und begreifen.

216

215 The liberation of Dachau.
216 After the liberation of Bergen-Belsen, the camp where Anne and Margot Frank died, the barracks are set afire to eliminate the spread of typhoid fever.
217 Temporary repatriation camps are set up in hotels and schools.

215 Die Befreiung Dachaus.
216 Im befreiten Bergen-Belsen – hier starben Anne und Margot Frank – werden die Baracken wegen der bestehenden Typhusgefahr niedergebrannt.
217 Für die Überlebenden werden in Hotels, Schulen und anderen Unterkünften Auffanglager eingerichtet.

217

53 A WORLD DIVIDED: THE POSTWAR YEARS

53 EINE GETEILTE WELT. DIE JAHRE NACH DEM KRIEG

The first photographs of the concentration camps cause a tremendous shock everywhere – how could a thing like this happen?

Twenty-two of the most important Nazi leaders are tried by the International Tribunal in Nuremberg in 1946. New legal principles are drafted there to prevent similar atrocities in the future. Another important document is the 'Universal Declaration of Human Rights,' adopted in 1948 by the United Nations, which was founded in 1945.

But the hope for international cooperation and justice doesn't last long. Soon after World War II, an ideological struggle occurs between the two former Allies, the United States and the Soviet Union: the Cold War. International politics have been dominated by the threat of an atomic war between the two superpowers ever since.

Die ersten Fotos aus den Konzentrationslagern verursachen auf der ganzen Welt einen Schock- wie konnte so etwas um Gottes Willen geschehen? 22 der wichtigsten Führungsmänner der Nazis stehen 1946 vor dem Internationalen Tribunal vor Gericht. Hier entstehen Rechtsnormen, die eine Wiederholung der Naziverbrechen unmöglich machen sollen. Ein wichtiges Dokument ist die 'Erklärung der Menschenrechte', die 1948 von den Vereinten Nationen, Gründungsjahr 1945, verabschiedet wird.

Aber die Hoffnung auf internationale Zusammenarbeit und Gerechtigkeit ist nur von kurzer Dauer. Zwischen den einstigen Bundgenossen USA und Sowjetunion bricht der 'Kalte Krieg' aus. Seither wird die internationale Politik von der drohenden Gefahr eines Atomkriegs überschattet.

218 *During the International Tribunal. Nuremberg, 1946.*
219 *Bergen-Belsen.*

218 *Während des Internationalen Militärtribunals in Nürnberg, 1946.*
219 *Bergen-Belsen.*

219

54 THE PUBLICATION OF ANNE FRANK'S DIARY

54 DER VERÖFFENTLICHUNG DES TAGEBUCHES DER ANNE FRANK

Upon his return to Amsterdam, Otto Frank realizes he is the only survivor of his family. Soon thereafter, Miep Gies gives Anne's papers and writings to him. After the people in hiding had been taken away, the helpers return to the Annex and take as much as possible before the Annex is cleared. Miep has kept Anne's papers during that time. Friends persuade Otto Frank to publish Anne's diary. 'The Diary of Anne Frank' appears in 1947 under the title 'Het Achterhuis' ('The Annex'). To date, more than 50 different editions have appeared, and more than 18 million copies have been sold. In 1953 Otto Frank marries Elfriede Markovits, also a survivor of Auschwitz. They settle in Basel, Switzerland, where Otto Frank dies in August 1980, at the age of 91.

The house where Anne and the others lived in hiding is now a museum, operated by the Anne Frank Foundation, which was founded in 1957. Apart from the preservation of the Annex, the Foundation tries to stimulate the fight against anti-Semitism, racism and fascism with information and educational projects.

Als Otto Frank nach Amsterdam zurückkehrt, wird ihm deutlich, dass er der einzige Überlebende der Familie ist. Schon nach kurzer Zeit überreicht Miep Gies ihm Annes Tagebücher, die sie die ganze Zeit über aufbewahrt hatte. Vor der Räumung des Hauses hatte sie es in Sicherheit gebracht. Auf Anraten von Freunden beschliesst Otto Frank, Annes Tagebuch zu veröffentlichen. 1947 erscheint die erste Auflage unter dem Titel 'Het Achterhuis' (Das Hinterhaus). Seither ist das Tagebuch in mehr als 50 Sprachen übersetzt und 18 millionenfach gedruckt worden. 1953 heiratet Otto Frank zum zweiten Mal. Mit seiner neuen Frau zieht er nach Basel. Dort stirbt Otto Frank 1980.

Seit 1957 ist das Anne Frank Haus ein Museum, das durch die Anne Frank Stiftung geführt wird. Neben der Museumsarbeit beschäftigt sich die Stiftung auch mit Bildungsarbeit und dem Erstellen von Unterrichtsmaterialien, um so einen Beitrag im Kampf gegen Antisemitismus, Rassismus und Faschismus zu leisten.

220 Otto Frank remarries in Amsterdam. His new wife is Elfriede Markovits. November 10, 1953.

220 Am 10. November 1953 heiratet Otto Frank in zweiter Ehe Elfriede Markovits, Amsterdam.

119.

Zaterdag 12 Feb. 1944.

Lieve Kitty,

De zon schijnt, de hemel is diep-blauw,
er waait een heerlijke wind en ik verlang, zo verlang ik naar alles .....
..... naar praten, naar vrijheid, naar
vrienden, naar alleen-zijn. Ik verlang
zo ..... naar huilen! Ik heb een gevoel in
me of ik spring en ik weet dat het met
huilen beter zou worden; ik kan het
niet. Ik ben onrustig loop van de ene naar
de andere kamer, adem door de kier van
een dicht raam, voel m'n hart kloppen,
alsof het zegt: "Vold'dat toch eindelijk
aan m'n verlangen."

Ik geloof dat ik het voorjaar in me
voel, ik voel het lente-ontwaken, ik voel
het in m'n hele lichaam en in m'n
ziel. Ik moet me in bedwang houden
om gewoon te doen, ik ben totaal in
de war, weet niet wat te lezen, wat
te schrijven, wat te doen, weet alleen
dat ik verlang .....

Je Anne.

286

221 Part of Anne's Diary
222 Cover of the first Dutch edition
of Anne's Diary

221 Fragment des Tagebuches.
222 Umschlag der ersten
niederländische Ausgabe von Anne
Franks Tagebuch.

222

221

55 NEO-NAZIS AND THE DENIAL OF THE HOLOCAUST

55 NEO-NAZIS UND DIE VERLEUGNUNG DES 'HOLOCAUST'

Following the end of World War II in 1945, Nazism and fascism did not disappear. In a number of countries small groups soon emerged and their ideas and appearance bore a great similarity to the old movement. Moreover, countless people who supported the Nazi regime were allowed to live in complete freedom and re-establish themselves in society. A small number of organizations openly admit their sympathy for fascism in its old form, and they deny its crimes. 'The Hoax of the 20th Century' is how Neo-Nazi groups label the mass murder of Jews by the Nazis. By denying the crimes of Nazi Germany, they try to rehabilitate National Socialism. Sometimes this takes the form of a so-called objective, historical discussion that does in no way remind us of uniformed Nazi groups and therefore is even more dangerous. To augment their following and to acquire a base of political support, these groups try to be accepted as honest, civil organizations.

Die Ideen der Nazis sind nach 1945 noch nicht tot. Schon kurze Zeit nach dem Krieg entstehen in verschiedenen Ländern Organisationen, die hinsichtlich ihrer Ideen und Darstellung den alten Bewegungen sehr nahe stehen. Viele Ex-Nazis bewegen sich ungestraft umher und können sich eine neue gesellschaftliche Position erwerben. Eine kleine Zahl von Gruppen gibt seine Symphatien für den alten Faschismus offen zu und leugnet die Verbrechen. 'Die Lüge des Jahrhunderts', so wird der Massenmord an den Juden in solchen Kreisen genannt. Indem man versucht, die Verbrechen des Hitler-Deutschlands zu vertuschen, hofft man, den Nationalsozialismus zu rehabilitieren. Manchmal geschieht das unter dem Deckmantel einer wertfreien, wissenschaftlichen Diskussion, die nichts mit den uniformierten Nazigruppen zu tun haben scheint. Aber gerade darum sind sie umso gefährlicher. Um ihre Anhängerschaft zu vergrössern, versuchen diese Gruppen sich als gemässigt, bürgerlich und ordentlich zu präsentieren.

223 The defaced barrack of the former Flossenburg concentration camp, April 1983: 'Wiesenthal is a Jewish liar, down with the concentration camp lies.'

224 German Neo-Nazis with posters: "I, ass, still believe that Jews were 'gassed' in German concentration camps."

223 Diese Baracke im ehemaligen Konzentrationslager Flossenbürg wurde mit einer Parole beschmiert, April 1983.

224 Deutsche Neo-Nazis mit Tafeln: "Ich Esel glaube noch, daß in deutsche KZ's Juden 'vergast' wurden".

Recently, violent anti-Semitic actions have spread fear among the Jewish community in Western Europe. For many it is an unbearable idea that 40 years after the end of World War II Jewish organizations are forced to use safety measures and ask for police support.

Apart from hard, violent anti-Semitism that reminds us of the hate against Jews during World War II, anti-Semitism sometimes takes the form of anti-Zionism. It is not always clear at what point anti-Zionism becomes anti-Semitism. Anti-Zionism rejects the state of Israel as a Jewish state, which is not the same as criticizing certain policies of the Israeli government. Often, however, one can surmise that criticism of the Israeli government is, in fact, based on the denial of the right of the state of Israel to exist as a Jewish state.

Compared to other states, isn't Israel judged by different standards, and if so, how has that come about? When the Israeli government takes action, not only the government is judged but all Jews everywhere are held responsible. In this way criticism of the state of Israel is used as justification for anti-Semitism.

In den lezten Jahren haben antisemitische Terroranschläge zu grosser Verunsicherung innerhalb der jüdischen Gemeinschaft Westeuropas geführt. 40 Jahre nach dem Krieg ist es für viele ein unerträglicher Gedanke, dass jüdische Einrichtungen gezwungen sind, Polizeischutz zu erbitten und andere Sicherheitsmassnahmen zu treffen.

Neben dem gewalttätigen Antisemitismus, der stark an den Judenhass im Zweiten Weltkrieg erinnert, gibt es noch den Antizionismus. Aber oft ist die Grenze zwischen Antizionismus und Antisemitismus nicht einfach zu erkennen. Antizionismus bedeutet das nicht Anerkennen Israels als jüdischen Staat. Das ist etwas ganz anderes, als Kritik an der Politik der Israelischen Regierung zu äussern. Oft entsteht der Eindruck, dass jedoch die wirklichen Motive für Kritik an der israelischen Regierung in der Aberkennung des Existenzrechtes des jüdischen Staates Israel begründet liegen. Wird der Staat Israel etwa mit anderen Massstäben gemessen als andere Länder, und wenn ja, woran liegt das?

An den Taten der israelischen Regierung werden nicht nur die Verantwortlichen, sondern oft alle Juden gemessen, ja sogar die, die überhaupt nicht in Israel leben. Zwar fühlen sich viele Juden auf der Welt mit Israel verbunden, es wäre aber völlig falsch, Kritik an der israelischen Politik in eine antijüdische Haltung umzusetzen. Auf diese Weise wird der Staat Israel benutzt, um Antisemitismus zu rechtfertigen.

225 Antwerp, Belgium. 1982.
226 At least two men open fire in Goldenberg's, a Jewish-owned restaurant in Paris. Six are killed, 22 are wounded. After the incident the owner of the restaurant, Jo Goldenberg, is about to collapse. August 9, 1982.

225 Antwerpen, 1982.
226 Am Mittag des 9. August 1982 schiessen mindestens zwei Männer mit Maschinenpistolen blind auf die Gäste im jüdischen Restaurant Goldenberg in Paris. Dabei sterben 6 Menschen und 22 andere werden verletzt. Der Besitzer, Jo Goldenberg, ist nach dem Attentat dem Zusammenbruch nahe.

225

140

Apart from Neo-Nazi groups, Europe is again confronted with racism. This is illustrated by an increasing number of violent racist incidents. Now that prosperity has ceased to grow and even threatens to decline, tolerance is put under pressure. This phenomenon is evident in all countries with ethnic minorities. Racial prejudices that already existed, in combination with the social-economic crisis, provide fertile soil for racism. The foreigner – that is to say, the identifiable 'colored' foreigner – is blamed for all the country's problems. If they would just leave, all the misery would disappear immediately, you can hear people say. Racist propaganda circulates in all countries in Western Europe, and the number of parties using this propaganda is increasing rapidly.
It is very important to fight discrimination. Therefore, it is a positive development that in those countries where racist groups are looking for support, many people are also fighting prejudice and racism.

Neben dem Neo-Nazismus ist in Europa auch die Rede von wachsendem Rassismus. Das lässt sich aus der steigenden Zahl gewalttätiger Vorfälle mit rassistischem Hintergrund ablesen. Der Wohlstand nimmt überall ab, und es droht noch schlimmer zu werden, was sich negativ auf Toleranz auswirkt. Alle Länder, in denen Minderheiten leben, kennen diese Erscheinung. Schon bestehende Vorurteile Menschen mit einer anderen Hautfarbe oder anderen Lebensgewohnheiten gegenüber bilden in Zeiten einer Wirtschatsflaute einen wichtigen Nährboden für Rassismus. Der Ausländer, und hier ist der an seiner Hautfarbe deutlich erkennbare gemeint, bekommt die Schuld an der Krise zugeschoben. Wenn er und die anderen verschwinden würden, käme das Ende der Krise, hört man Rassisten oft beteuern.
Diese rassistische Propaganda wird in ganz Europa verbreitet. Die Zahl der Gruppen, die sich dieser Parolen bedient, nimmt in letzter Zeit zu. Es ist sehr wichtig, dass Diskriminierung bekämpft wird. Darum ist es erfreulich, dass sich in den Ländern, in denen sich rassistischen Grupierungen um Anhängerschaft bemühen, besonders viele sich im Kampf gegen Rassismus und Diskriminierung engagieren.

227 In France Le Pen's Front National achieved 11% of the vote in the 1984 election. His party mainly focuses on blaming foreign workers for the economic crisis.
228 International Day Against Racism. This woman is carrying photographs of victims of racist violence in France. March 21, 1984.
229 The hate campaign against foreigners conducted in the 'Deutsche National Zeitung,' Germany. 'Who will save us from the immigrants?' 'Is Germany to become a second Turkey?' 'Our people are in danger!'
230 'Immigrant workers, go home!' The Vlaamse Militanten Orde (Flemish Militant Order) demonstrating in Antwerp, Belgium. December 1982.

Wer rettet uns vor den Ausländern?

Beherrschen Ausländer bald völlig unser Land?

Damm gegen Ausländerflut

Ausländer — Gefahr für Deutschland

Werden die Deutschen an die Wand gedrückt?/S. 3

Sind die Ausländer

Millionen Ausländer zuviel

noch zu stoppen?

Die Ursachen der Arbeitslosigkeit

Wie Millionen Türken

Sollen Ausländer

Deutschland überfremden

Deutsche werden?

Wahnsinnspläne in Bonn

Unser Volk in Gefahr

Wie kriminelle Ausländer

uns alle bedrohen

Asylbetrüger – Rauschgifthändler

Wie Bundesinnenminister Baum ausländische Verbrecher schützt

Was uns die Ausländer kosten

Wird Deutschland

Wie Millionen Ausländer

zur zweiten Türkei?

Deutschland überfremden

Millionen Türken im Anmarsch

Wann haben die Ausländer

Wie die Ausländer
...erober...

228

229

227 In Frankreich erzielt die
'Front National' unter der Führung
von Le Pen 1984 unerwartet hohe
Wahlergebnisse. Zu den
wichtigsten
Wahlprogrammpunkten gehörte:
Die Gastarbeiter sind Schuld an der
Wirtschaftkrise.
228 21. März 1984. Internationaler
Tag gegen Rassismus. Diese Frau
trägt Fotos von Opfern rassistischer
Gewalt in Frankreich bei sich.
229 Hetze gegen Ausländer in der
'Deutschen National Zeitung'.
230 'Gastarbeiter raus'. Der
'Flämische Militante Orden'
demonstriert im belgischen
Antwerpen, Dezember 1983.

230

COLOPHON

This book was produced on the occasion of the exhibition, 'Anne Frank in the world, 1929–1945'.
Photo research and text: Joke Kniesmeyer, Dienke Hondius, Bauco van der Wal.
Research concerning Frankfurt provided by: Dr. Jürgen Steen, Historisches Museum, Frankfurt.
English language text provided by: Steven Arthur Cohen, Amsterdam.
Cover-design: Marius van Leeuwen, Amsterdam.
Graphic design and layout: Marius van Leeuwen and Nel Punt, Amsterdam.
Typeset and printed by: Veenman, Wageningen.

KOLOPHON

Buch zur Ausstellung 'Die Welt der Anne Frank, 1929–1945'.
Bildredaktion und Text: Joke Kniesmeyer, Dienke Hondius, Bauco van der Wal.
Recherchen über Frankfurt: Dr. Jürgen Steen, Historisches Museum, Frankfurt.
Deutsche Übersetzung: Alex Suijk, Johannes Kaiser.
Umschlagentwurf: Marius van Leeuwen.
Lay-out: Marius van Leeuwen, Nel Punt, Amsterdam.
Satz und Druck: Veenman, Wageningen.